KETO *Diet*
Cookbook
for Beginners

150 Delicious and Simple Resipes with Low Carbs and Sugar.
Lose Weight Effortlessly, Give Energy and Change your
Health with the 30-Day Meal Plan

ADAM PIERCE

Table of contentsc

CHAPTER 4

BEEF, LAMB & PORK 67

CHAPTER 5

FISH & SEAFOOD 88

CHAPTER 6

SPICY (EXOTIC) RECIPES 103

CHAPTER 1

Advantages of the keto diet

The ketogenic diet, commonly known as the keto diet, is a low-carbohydrate, high-fat diet that has gained popularity for its potential health benefits.

Here are some of the key benefits associated with the keto diet:

1. **Weight Loss:** One of the primary reasons people adopt the keto diet is for weight loss. By significantly reducing carbohydrate intake and replacing it with fats, the body enters a state of ketosis, where it burns fat for fuel instead of carbohydrates. This can lead to rapid weight loss for many individuals.

2. **Improved Blood Sugar Control:** For some people, especially those with type 2 diabetes, the keto diet can help stabilize blood sugar levels. The reduced carbohydrate intake leads to lower blood sugar spikes and improved insulin sensitivity.

3. **Improved Mental Focus and Clarity:** Some individuals on the keto diet experience improved cognitive function, including better focus and mental clarity. This is thought to be related to the brain's use of ketones for energy, which may provide a more stable fuel source compared to glucose.

4. **Appetite Suppression:** The high-fat content of the keto diet, combined with adequate protein intake, can help keep you feeling full and satisfied, reducing hunger and cravings. This can make it easier to adhere to a calorie-restricted diet, leading to further weight loss.

5. **Better Cholesterol Levels:** Contrary to common belief, the keto diet can actually improve cholesterol levels for many people. It tends to increase HDL (good) cholesterol while decreasing LDL (bad) cholesterol and triglycerides, which can reduce the risk of heart disease.

6. **Potential Therapeutic Applications:** The keto diet has been used since the 1920s to treat epilepsy, particularly among children who do not respond well to anti-epileptic drugs. It is also being studied for other neurological disorders, such as Alzheimer's disease and Parkinson's disease.

It's important to note that the keto diet may not be suitable for everyone, and it can have side effects, especially during the initial phase when the body is adjusting to a new fuel source. Common side effects include the "keto flu," which is characterized by headaches, fatigue, nausea, and irritability. Additionally, because the diet is restrictive, it can lead to deficiencies in certain nutrients if not carefully planned. Always consider consulting with a healthcare provider or a dietitian before starting a new diet.

Ketosis and ketoacidosis

Ketosis is a metabolic state where your body burns fat for fuel instead of carbohydrates.

Normally, your body converts carbohydrates into glucose, which is used as the primary source of energy. However, when carbohydrate intake is restricted, such as during fasting or following a low-carbohydrate diet like the ketogenic diet, the body starts breaking down fat stores into molecules called ketones. These ketones can then be used by the body and the brain as an alternative fuel source.

Ketosis is sometimes sought after for weight loss, as it indicates that the body is burning fat. It's also the basis for ketogenic diets, which are used not only for weight loss but also for managing certain medical conditions like epilepsy.

However, it's important to distinguish between ketosis and ketoacidosis, the latter being a dangerous condition often associated with diabetes, where ketone levels become excessively high.

Ketoacidosis is a serious metabolic complication that can occur in people with diabetes, particularly those with type 1 diabetes. It happens when there's a significant lack of insulin in the body, leading to high levels of ketones and blood sugar.

In ketoacidosis, the accumulation of ketones in the blood leads to a decrease in blood pH, resulting in a state of metabolic acidosis. Symptoms of ketoacidosis can include extreme thirst, frequent urination, nausea, vomiting, abdominal pain, weakness, confusion, and a fruity-scented breath. If left untreated, it can lead to severe dehydration, and even coma.

Ketoacidosis requires immediate medical attention and is treated with fluids, electrolytes, and insulin to correct the high blood sugar levels and restore the body's normal acid-base balance. It's crucial for individuals with diabetes to monitor their blood sugar levels and ketone levels regularly to prevent this condition.

Keto diet without fanaticism or metabolic flexibility

Keto adaptation, refers to the process by which the body adjusts to a ketogenic diet, which is high in fats and low in carbohydrates.

This dietary shift causes the body to switch its primary source of energy from glucose (derived from carbohydrates) to ketones, which are compounds produced through the breakdown of fats in the liver. This adjustment period is critical as it involves physiological changes that enable the efficient utilization of ketone bodies for energy by the brain, muscles, and other tissues.

During ketoadaptation, individuals may experience a variety of symptoms known as the "keto flu," which can include fatigue, headaches, nausea, and irritability. These symptoms typically resolve within a few days to weeks as the body becomes more efficient at producing and using ketones. Once adapted, many report increased energy levels, reduced appetite, and improved mental clarity.

Ketoadaptation is the initial stage towards achieving metabolic flexibility.

Metabolic flexibility is the capacity of the body to adapt fuel oxidation to fuel availability. This means the body can efficiently switch between burning carbohydrates and fats depending on what's available. For instance, after a high-carbohydrate meal, a metabolically flexible person can quickly switch to burning glucose. Conversely, when fasting or during low carbohydrate intake, the same person can efficiently switch to burning fat.

Let's get the main thing straight: the goal of the keto diet is not ketosis, but health and metabolic flexibility.

This is the ability to switch from one type of fuel (ketones) to another (glucose) and back again without any unpleasant sensations or health consequences. As, in fact, our ancient ancestors did. It is unlikely that any of them, having found a nest of wild bees, froze in thoughts like: "Can I eat honey? No, I won't, it will knock me out of ketosis." Metabolic flexibility is what is inherent in a healthy body. At the same time, no one is suggesting that you return to cakes and oatmeal. On the contrary, in order to maintain this flexibility for many years and from time to time to afford frank excesses, it is necessary that the general line remains unchanged: many fats, moderate proteins and few carbohydrates.

Checklist "How to determine ketosis"

A checklist to help determine if you're in ketosis without using devices might include monitoring various physical symptoms and signs.

It's important to remember, however, that these indicators are not as accurate as using devices like ketone meters or test strips. Here's a simple checklist you can follow:

- ✓ **you have stopped pouncing on food and do not feel the painful feeling of hunger;**

- ✓ **lose weight without counting calories;**

- ✓ **you are very energetic;**

- ✓ **you think faster and more clearly;**

- ✓ **improved memory;**

- ✓ **you forgot about heartburn;**

- ✓ **blood sugar normalized;**

- ✓ **you get sick less;**

- ✓ **got rid of allergies and asthma;**

- ✓ **you sleep better;**

- ✓ **your skin has improved, you have become younger;**

- ✓ **you do not feel bloated after eating;**

- ✓ **you have become more emotionally stable;**

- ✓ **you have disappeared or have become very rare migraines.**

How to survive the keto flu

Ideological enemies of the keto diet describe keto flu as an incurable disease. You will be persuaded that without it, the transition to keto is impossible "giving birth is easier than surviving keto flu."☺ It is not true.

If you do everything gradually, carefully and wisely, then you may not feel the keto flu. The main thing is not to focus on it and not to wait for it with fear, because we know that fear is a great power.

Keto flu is a common experience some people go through when they start the ketogenic diet. It's a collection of symptoms that can feel similar to the flu and occurs as your body adjusts to using fat instead of carbohydrates as its primary energy source.

Here are some strategies to help manage or reduce the symptoms of keto flu:

1. **STAY HYDRATED:**

   • The shift to a ketogenic diet can lead to dehydration and electrolyte imbalances, so it's important to drink plenty of water. You might also need to increase your intake of salts, such as sodium, potassium, and magnesium, to help retain water and reduce symptoms like headaches or fatigue.

2. **REPLACE ELECTROLYTES:**

   • Along with staying hydrated, replenishing electrolytes is crucial. Consider adding a little extra salt to your meals or drinking broth. Supplements for potassium and magnesium might also be helpful, but it's best to consult with a healthcare provider before starting any supplements.

3. **EASE INTO THE DIET**

   • Instead of drastically reducing carbohydrate intake overnight, you might find it easier to slowly reduce carbs over a few weeks. This gradual approach can help your body adjust more smoothly.

4. **EAT ENOUGH FAT AND CALORIES:**

   • Make sure you're not undereating. Adequate caloric intake from healthy fats is essential on the ketogenic diet. Foods like avocados, nuts, seeds, and olive oil are good sources of healthy fats. For those on a ketogenic diet, drinks like bulletproof coffee and keto candies like fat bombs can provide healthy fats. A spoonful of coconut oil can also be a good option.

5. GET PLENTY OF SLEEP:

- Lack of sleep can worsen the symptoms of keto flu. Try to maintain good sleep hygiene by keeping a regular sleep schedule, creating a restful environment, and avoiding caffeine late in the day.

6. MANAGE STRESS:

- High stress can exacerbate keto flu symptoms. Activities like meditation, walking, or yoga can help manage stress levels.

7. CONSIDER EXOGENOUS KETONES:

- These are supplements that provide ketone bodies which your body can use for energy before it becomes efficient at producing them itself. They might help alleviate some symptoms by providing an alternative energy source.

8. STAY ACTIVE, BUT DON'T OVERDO IT:

- Light activity, like walking or gentle yoga, can help your body adjust. Avoid intense workouts during the first few weeks as your body is adapting.

These tips can help make the transition to a ketogenic diet more comfortable. However, if symptoms persist or you have concerns about your health while following the ketogenic diet, it's important to consult a healthcare provider.

Because we are all different, our psychological and moral states vary. Some are more resilient and can easily manage transitions, while others may find it harder. Some have poorer health and need to be more careful in choosing their diet, while others will not fuss about a meal plan and will simply cut out carbohydrates without even feeling it. It's similar to smoking—some quit smoking in one day and everything is fine, while others feel so bad that 'their ears curl up' ;) In any case, hang in there and don't give up—you will succeed.

CHAPTER 2

Breakfast Recipes

Spinach, Mushrooms, Tomatoes, Avocado, and Scrambled Eggs

Yield:
Serves 2

Prep Time:
10 minutes

Cook Time:
10 minutes

Total Time:
20 minutes

Nutritional Information
(per serving):

🔥 **Calories: 320**

Fat: 25g
Carbohydrates: 9g
(Net Carbs: 4g)
Fiber: 5g
Protein: 14g

Ingredients:

4 large eggs
1 cup fresh spinach, roughly chopped
1/2 cup mushrooms, sliced
1/2 cup cherry tomatoes, halved
1 ripe avocado, peeled and sliced

2 tablespoons olive oil
Salt and pepper, to taste
Optional: shredded cheese or herbs such as chives for garnish

1. **Prep the Ingredients:**
   - Wash and chop the spinach, slice the mushrooms, halve the tomatoes, and slice the avocado. Set aside.

2. **Cook Vegetables:**
   - In a non-stick skillet, heat 1 tablespoon of olive oil over medium heat. Add the mushrooms and sauté for about 3 minutes until they begin to soften. Add the cherry tomatoes and spinach, cooking until the spinach wilts, about 2 minutes. Remove from heat and set aside.

3. **Scramble the Eggs:**
   - In a bowl, whisk the eggs with salt and pepper. Heat the remaining tablespoon of olive oil in the same skillet. Pour in the eggs and let them sit, undisturbed, for about 1 minute. Then, gently stir with a spatula until they just set but remain slightly runny in texture.

4. **Combine and Serve:**
   - Add the sautéed vegetables back to the skillet with the eggs. Gently fold to combine. Remove from heat. Serve the scramble with sliced avocado on top and garnish with optional cheese or herbs.

Turkey Bacon & Spinach Crepes

Yield:
Serves 4

Prep Time:
15 minutes

Cook Time:
20 minutes

Total Time:
35 minutes

Nutritional Information
(per serving):

🔥 **Calories: 340**

Fat: 26g
Carbohydrates: 8g
(Net Carbs: 4g)
Fiber: 4g
Protein: 21g

Ingredients:

For the Crepes:
4 large eggs
1/4 cup almond flour
1/4 cup coconut flour
1/2 cup water
2 tablespoons melted butter
Pinch of salt

For the Filling:
8 slices turkey bacon, chopped
2 cups fresh spinach
1/2 cup shredded cheese (cheddar or mozzarella)
1 tablespoon olive oil
Salt and pepper, to taste

1. **Make the Crepes:**
   - In a blender, combine the eggs, almond flour, coconut flour, water, melted butter, and salt. Blend until smooth.
   - Heat a non-stick skillet over medium heat and lightly grease with butter or oil. Pour about 1/4 cup of the batter into the skillet, swirling to spread evenly. Cook for 2-3 minutes until the edges lift easily, then flip and cook for another 1-2 minutes. Set aside and repeat with the remaining batter.

2. **Prepare the Filling:**
   - In the same skillet, cook the turkey bacon until crispy. Remove and set aside.
   - In the residual bacon fat, add olive oil if needed, and sauté the spinach until wilted. Season with salt and pepper.

3. **Assemble the Crepes:**
   - Lay out the crepes and distribute the cooked spinach and crispy turkey bacon evenly among them. Sprinkle cheese over each.
   - Fold the crepes in half, then fold again to form triangles, or roll them up.
   - Return the filled crepes to the skillet, and cook on each side for about 1 minute or until the cheese is melted and the crepes are heated through.

Eggs with Prosciutto-Wrapped Asparagus

Yield:
Serves 2

Prep Time:
10 minutes

Cook Time:
20 minutes

Total Time:
30 minutes

Nutritional Information
(per serving):

🔥 **Calories: 310**

Fat: 23g
Carbohydrates: 3g
(Net Carbs: 2g)
Fiber: 1g
Protein: 22g

Ingredients:

8 asparagus spears, trimmed

4 slices of prosciutto

4 large eggs

1 tablespoon white vinegar

2 tablespoons olive oil

Salt and pepper, to taste

Optional garnishes: shaved Parmesan cheese, fresh herbs (such as parsley or chives)

1. **Prepare the Asparagus:**
   - Preheat your oven to 400°F (200°C).
   - Wrap each asparagus spear with half a slice of prosciutto, covering most of the spear but leaving the tips exposed.
   - Place the wrapped asparagus on a baking sheet lined with parchment paper. Drizzle with olive oil and season with a little pepper.
   - Roast in the preheated oven for about 15-20 minutes, or until the asparagus is tender and the prosciutto is crispy.

2. **Poach the Eggs:**
   - Fill a medium saucepan with about 3 inches of water and add the white vinegar. Bring to a gentle simmer.
   - Crack each egg into a small cup or bowl. Gently slide the eggs into the simmering water, one at a time.
   - Cook for about 3-4 minutes, or until the whites are set but the yolks are still runny. Remove with a slotted spoon and drain on a paper towel.

3. **Serve:**
   - Arrange two poached eggs on each plate. Add four prosciutto-wrapped asparagus spears alongside each serving.
   - Optionally, garnish with shaved Parmesan and fresh herbs.

Chocolate Keto Omelet

Yield:
Serves 1

Prep Time:
5 minutes

Cook Time:
5 minutes

Total Time:
10 minutes

Nutritional Information
(per serving, without toppings):

🔥 Calories: 300

Fat: 26g
Carbohydrates: 5g
(Net Carbs: 3g)
Fiber: 2g
Protein: 13g

Ingredients:

2 large eggs

1 tablespoon unsweetened cocoa powder

1 tablespoon erythritol (or another keto-friendly sweetener)

1/4 teaspoon vanilla extract

1 tablespoon heavy cream

1 tablespoon butter

Optional toppings: sugar-free chocolate chips, whipped cream, fresh berries

1. **Prepare the Egg Mixture:**
   - In a small bowl, whisk together the eggs, cocoa powder, erythritol, vanilla extract, and heavy cream until well combined and slightly frothy.

2. **Cook the Omelet:**
   - Heat butter in a non-stick skillet over medium heat. Once the butter is melted and hot, pour in the egg mixture.
   - Cook for about 2 minutes, or until the edges start to lift from the pan. Use a spatula to gently lift the edges and tilt the pan to allow the uncooked egg to flow underneath.
   - Once the top is nearly set, carefully fold the omelet in half, and continue to cook for another minute.

3. **Serve:**
   - Slide the omelet onto a plate and add any optional toppings like sugar-free chocolate chips, a dollop of whipped cream, or fresh berries.

Cheese and Onion Cheesecakes

Yield:
Makes 12 mini cheesecakes

Prep Time:
15 minutes

Cook Time:
25 minutes

Total Time:
40 minutes

Nutritional Information
(per cheesecake):

🔥 **Calories: 230**

Fat: 20g
Carbohydrates: 4g
(Net Carbs: 2g)
Fiber: 2g
Protein: 8g

Ingredients:

For the Crust:

1 cup almond flour

1/3 cup grated Parmesan cheese

3 tablespoons melted butter

1/2 teaspoon garlic powder

Salt, to taste

For the Filling:

2 cups cream cheese, softened

1 cup shredded cheddar cheese

1 large egg

1/2 cup caramelized onions
(about 1 large onion, thinly sliced and cooked slowly in 2 tablespoons butter until golden)

1/2 teaspoon black pepper

1/4 teaspoon salt

1 tablespoon chives, chopped
(for garnish)

1. **Prepare the Crust:**
   - Preheat your oven to 350°F (175°C).
   - In a bowl, mix together almond flour, grated Parmesan, melted butter, garlic powder, and a pinch of salt until well combined.
   - Divide the mixture among 12 mini muffin tins or mini cheesecake pans, pressing firmly to form a crust at the bottom of each.
   - Bake for 5 minutes, then remove from the oven and set aside to cool slightly.

2. **Make the Filling:**
   - In a mixing bowl, blend the cream cheese, cheddar cheese, egg, caramelized onions, black pepper, and salt until smooth and well combined.
   - Spoon the cheese mixture over the crusts in the mini muffin tins, filling each one almost to the top.

3. **Bake the Cheesecakes:**
   - Return the filled tins to the oven and bake for 20 minutes, or until the filling is set and the edges are lightly browned.
   - Remove from the oven and allow to cool for 5 minutes, then carefully remove each cheesecake from the tin.

4. **Serve:**
   - Garnish with chopped chives before serving. These can be enjoyed warm or at room temperature.

Almond Keto Porridge

Yield:
Serves 2

Prep Time:
5 minutes

Cook Time:
10 minutes

Total Time:
15 minutes

Nutritional Information
(per serving, without toppings):

🔥 Calories: 280

Fat: 23g
Carbohydrates: 12g
(Net Carbs: 4g)
Fiber: 8g
Protein: 7g

Ingredients:

1/2 cup almond flour

1/4 cup shredded unsweetened coconut

1 tablespoon flaxseed meal

1 tablespoon chia seeds

1 cup unsweetened almond milk

1/4 teaspoon cinnamon

1/4 teaspoon vanilla extract

Sweetener of choice (e.g., erythritol, stevia) to taste

Optional toppings: sliced almonds, fresh berries, or a dollop of keto-friendly yogurt

1. **Mix Ingredients:**

   • In a small saucepan, combine the almond flour, shredded coconut, flaxseed meal, and chia seeds. Mix well to distribute evenly.

2. **Cook the Porridge:**

   • Stir in the almond milk, cinnamon, and vanilla extract. Bring the mixture to a low simmer over medium heat, stirring frequently to prevent sticking.

   • Cook for about 5-7 minutes, or until the porridge thickens to your desired consistency. Adjust the sweetness to your taste by adding your chosen sweetener.

3. **Serve:**

   • Divide the porridge into bowls. Add any optional toppings like sliced almonds, fresh berries, or a spoonful of keto-friendly yogurt.

   • Serve hot for a comforting and filling breakfast.

Frittata with Goat Cheese and Mushrooms

Yield:
Serves 4

Prep Time:
10 minutes

Cook Time:
20 minutes

Total Time:
30 minutes

Nutritional Information
(per serving):

🔥 **Calories: 390**

Fat: 32g
Carbohydrates: 5g
(Net Carbs: 4g)
Fiber: 1g
Protein: 20g

Ingredients:

8 large eggs

1/2 cup heavy cream

4 ounces goat cheese, crumbled

1 cup mushrooms, sliced

1/2 medium onion, thinly sliced

2 tablespoons olive oil

Salt and pepper, to taste

Fresh herbs (such as thyme or parsley), for garnish

1. **Preheat and Prep:**
   - Preheat the oven to 375°F (190°C).
   - In a medium mixing bowl, whisk together the eggs and heavy cream. Season with salt and pepper. Stir in half of the crumbled goat cheese.

2. **Cook the Vegetables:**
   - Heat olive oil in an oven-safe skillet over medium heat. Add the sliced onions and mushrooms, sautéing until the onions are translucent and the mushrooms are browned and tender, about 5-7 minutes.

3. **Combine Ingredients:**
   - Pour the egg and cream mixture over the cooked mushrooms and onions in the skillet. Let it cook without stirring for about 2 minutes to allow the bottom to set slightly. Sprinkle the remaining goat cheese over the top.

4. **Bake the Frittata:**
   - Transfer the skillet to the preheated oven. Bake for 15-18 minutes, or until the eggs are fully set and the top is lightly golden.

5. **Serve:**
   - Remove from the oven and let it cool for a few minutes. Garnish with fresh herbs before slicing into wedges.

Avocado and Egg Salad

Yield:
Serves 4

Prep Time:
10 minutes

Cook Time:
10 minutes (for the eggs)

Total Time:
20 minutes

Nutritional Information
(per serving):

🔥 **Calories: 340**

Fat: 29g
Carbohydrates: 8g
(Net Carbs: 4g)
Fiber: 4g
Protein: 13g

Ingredients:

6 large eggs

2 ripe avocados, diced

1/4 cup mayonnaise
(preferably avocado oil mayo)

1 tablespoon Dijon mustard

1 tablespoon fresh lemon juice

1/4 cup finely chopped red onion

2 tablespoons chopped fresh cilantro
(or parsley)

Salt and pepper, to taste

Optional: 1 diced celery stalk for crunch

1. **Cook the Eggs:**
   - Place the eggs in a saucepan and cover with water. Bring to a boil over medium-high heat. Once boiling, cover the pan, turn off the heat, and let stand for 10 minutes.
   - After 10 minutes, drain the hot water and rinse the eggs under cold water to stop the cooking process. Peel the eggs once they are cool enough to handle.

2. **Prepare the Salad:**
   - In a large bowl, mash the peeled eggs with a fork or potato masher to your desired consistency.
   - Add the diced avocados, mayonnaise, Dijon mustard, lemon juice, red onion, and cilantro. If using, add the diced celery. Gently mix to combine all ingredients. Season with salt and pepper to taste.

3. **Serve:**
   - Serve immediately, or cover and refrigerate to let the flavors meld together. This salad can be served on its own, over a bed of greens, or with keto-friendly crackers.

Chia Seed Pudding

Yield:
Serves 2

Prep Time:
5 minutes (plus at least 2 hours for chilling)

Cook Time:
0 minutes

Total Time:
5 minutes

Nutritional Information
(per serving, without toppings):

🔥 **Calories: 140**

Fat: 9g
Carbohydrates: 12g
(Net Carbs: 2g)
Fiber: 10g
Protein: 5g

Ingredients:

1/4 cup chia seeds

1 cup unsweetened almond milk (or any keto-friendly milk alternative)

1/2 teaspoon vanilla extract

1 tablespoon erythritol or any other

keto-friendly sweetener

Optional toppings: unsweetened coconut flakes, nuts, keto-friendly granola, or fresh berries

1. **Mix the Pudding:**
   - In a bowl, combine the chia seeds, almond milk, vanilla extract, and sweetener. Stir well to mix everything evenly. Ensure there are no clumps of chia seeds stuck together.

2. **Chill:**
   - Cover the bowl with plastic wrap or transfer the mixture to a sealed container. Refrigerate for at least 2 hours, or overnight. This allows the chia seeds to absorb the liquid and swell, forming a gel-like consistency.

3. **Serve:**
   - Once the pudding has set and is thick, give it a good stir to break up any clumps. Divide the pudding into serving bowls or glasses.
   - Add optional toppings like coconut flakes, nuts, keto-friendly granola, or fresh berries before serving.

Keto Cauliflower Hash Browns

Yield:
Makes 8 hash browns

Prep Time:
15 minutes

Cook Time:
15 minutes

Total Time:
30 minutes

Nutritional Information
(per hash brown):

🔥 **Calories: 120**

Fat: 9g
Carbohydrates: 4g
(Net Carbs: 2g)
Fiber: 2g
Protein: 5g

Ingredients:

1 medium head cauliflower, grated or processed into rice-sized pieces

1/2 cup shredded cheese (cheddar works well)

1 large egg

1/4 cup almond flour

1/2 teaspoon garlic powder

Salt and pepper, to taste

2 tablespoons olive oil or avocado oil for frying

1. **Prepare the Cauliflower:**
   - Rinse the cauliflower and dry it thoroughly. Grate the cauliflower using a box grater or pulse it in a food processor until it resembles rice grains.
   - Transfer the grated cauliflower to a microwave-safe bowl, cover, and microwave for 4 minutes. Let it cool slightly, then wrap it in a clean kitchen towel and squeeze out as much moisture as possible.

2. **Mix Ingredients:**
   - In a large bowl, combine the dried cauliflower, shredded cheese, egg, almond flour, garlic powder, and a pinch of salt and pepper. Mix until everything is well incorporated.

3. **Form the Hash Browns:**
   - Divide the mixture into 8 equal portions. Shape each portion into a compact patty.

4. **Cook the Hash Browns:**
   - Heat the oil in a large skillet over medium heat. Once hot, add the hash brown patties and cook for about 5-7 minutes per side or until they are golden brown and crispy.

5. **Serve:**
   - Serve the hash browns hot, optionally topped with a dollop of sour cream or a sprinkle of fresh herbs.

Sausage and Pepper Skillet

Yield:
Serves 4

Prep Time:
10 minutes

Cook Time:
20 minutes

Total Time:
30 minutes

Nutritional Information
(per serving):

🔥 **Calories: 390**

Fat: 28g
Carbohydrates: 10g
(Net Carbs: 7g)
Fiber: 3g
Protein: 24g

Ingredients:

1 pound Italian sausages (choose a keto-friendly option without added sugars)

1 red bell pepper, sliced

1 green bell pepper, sliced

1 yellow bell pepper, sliced

1 onion, sliced

2 cloves garlic, minced

2 tablespoons olive oil

1 teaspoon dried oregano

1/2 teaspoon red pepper flakes (optional)

Salt and pepper, to taste

Fresh basil or parsley, for garnish

1. **Cook the Sausages:**
   - In a large skillet, heat 1 tablespoon of olive oil over medium heat. Add the sausages and cook until browned and cooked through, about 10 minutes. Remove sausages from the skillet and slice them into rounds.

2. **Sauté the Vegetables:**
   - In the same skillet, add the remaining olive oil. Add the onions and garlic and sauté for about 2 minutes until the onions start to soften.
   - Add the sliced bell peppers, dried oregano, red pepper flakes (if using), and a pinch of salt and pepper. Continue to cook, stirring occasionally, until the peppers are soft and slightly caramelized, about 8 minutes.

3. **Combine and Serve:**
   - Return the sliced sausages to the skillet with the vegetables and stir to combine. Cook for an additional 2-3 minutes to reheat the sausages and blend the flavors.
   - Garnish with chopped basil or parsley before serving.

Breakfast Sandwich

Yield:
Serves 2

Prep Time:
10 minutes

Cook Time:
15 minutes

Total Time:
25 minutes

Nutritional Information
(per serving):

🔥 **Calories: 540**

Fat: 45g
Carbohydrates: 2g
(Net Carbs: 2g)
Fiber: 0g
Protein: 33g

Ingredients:

4 large eggs

1/2 teaspoon baking powder

Salt and pepper, to taste

2 sausage patties (keto-friendly)

2 slices of cheddar cheese

1 tablespoon butter

Optional: slices of avocado or a smear of mayonnaise for extra fat

1. **Prepare the Egg Buns:**
   - In a bowl, whisk 2 eggs with baking powder, salt, and pepper until well combined.
   - Heat a non-stick skillet over medium heat and add half the butter. Pour half of the egg mixture into the skillet, forming a round shape similar to a pancake. Cook for about 2-3 minutes on each side or until fully set and golden. Repeat with the remaining eggs to make a second "bun."

2. **Cook the Sausage Patties:**
   - In the same skillet, cook the sausage patties over medium heat until browned and cooked through, about 5 minutes per side. Set aside.

3. **Assemble the Sandwich:**
   - Place a slice of cheese on one egg bun while it's still warm so the cheese begins to melt.
   - Add a cooked sausage patty on top of the cheese, then any additional toppings like avocado or mayonnaise if using.
   - Top with the second egg bun to complete the sandwich.

Herbed Buttery Breakfast Steak

Yield:
Serves 2

Prep Time:
5 minutes

Cook Time:
10 minutes

Total Time:
15 minutes

Nutritional Information
(per serving):

🔥 **Calories: 450**

Fat: 35g
Carbohydrates: 1g
(Net Carbs: 1g)
Fiber: 0g
Protein: 34g

Ingredients:

2 steaks (about 6 ounces each, such as sirloin or ribeye)

2 tablespoons butter

1 clove garlic, minced

1 tablespoon fresh herbs (such as parsley, thyme, or rosemary), finely chopped

Salt and pepper, to taste

1 tablespoon olive oil

1. **Prep the Herbed Butter:**
   - In a small bowl, mix the butter with the minced garlic and chopped herbs. Set aside at room temperature to allow the flavors to meld.

2. **Cook the Steaks:**
   - Season the steaks generously with salt and pepper.
   - Heat a skillet over medium-high heat and add olive oil. Once hot, add the steaks to the skillet.
   - Cook for about 4-5 minutes on each side for medium-rare, or adjust the cooking time to your desired doneness.
   - Remove the steaks from the skillet and let them rest for a few minutes.

3. **Serve:**
   - Top each steak with a dollop of the prepared herbed butter. Allow the butter to melt over the warm steaks.
   - Serve immediately while warm and buttery.

Savory Waffles with Cheese & Tomato

Yield:
Serves 4

Prep Time:
10 minutes

Cook Time:
20 minutes

Total Time:
30 minutes

Nutritional Information
(per serving):

🔥 **Calories: 350**

Fat: 28g
Carbohydrates: 12g
(Net Carbs: 7g)
Fiber: 5g
Protein: 15g

Ingredients:

1 cup almond flour
1/4 cup coconut flour
1 teaspoon baking powder
1/2 teaspoon garlic powder
1/2 teaspoon onion powder
Salt and pepper, to taste
2 large eggs

1/4 cup unsweetened almond milk
1/2 cup shredded mozzarella cheese
1/4 cup grated Parmesan cheese
1/4 cup sun-dried tomatoes, chopped
2 tablespoons fresh basil, chopped
2 tablespoons olive oil (for greasing tz iron)

1. **Mix Dry Ingredients:**
   - In a large mixing bowl, combine almond flour, coconut flour, baking powder, garlic powder, onion powder, salt, and pepper.

2. **Add Wet Ingredients:**
   - Whisk in the eggs and almond milk until the mixture is smooth.

3. **Add Cheese and Tomatoes:**
   - Fold in the mozzarella and Parmesan cheeses, sun-dried tomatoes, and chopped basil.

4. **Preheat Waffle Iron:**
   - Preheat your waffle iron according to the manufacturer's instructions and brush it with olive oil to prevent sticking.

5. **Cook the Waffles:**
   - Pour enough batter into the waffle iron to cover the grids (typically about 1/4 to 1/3 cup, depending on the size of your waffle iron). Close the lid and cook until the waffle is golden and crisp, about 5 minutes. Repeat with the remaining batter.

6. **Serve:**
   - Serve the waffles hot, optionally topped with additional fresh basil or a dollop of sour cream.

Keto Baked Avocado Eggs

Yield:
2 servings

Prep Time:
5 minutes

Cook Time:
15 minutes

Total Time:
20 minutes

Nutritional Information
(per serving, approximately):

🔥 **Calories: 470**

Fat: 40g
Protein: 18g
Carbohydrates: 12g
(Net carbs: 4g)
Fiber: 8g

Ingredients:
2 ripe avocados
4 small eggs
Salt and pepper, to taste

2 tablespoons chopped chives or green onions (for garnish)

1 tablespoon crumbled feta or goat cheese (optional)

Red pepper flakes (optional)

1. **Preheat the oven to 425°F (220°C).**

2. **Prepare the avocados:**
   - Slice the avocados in half and remove the pits. Use a spoon to scoop out a bit more avocado to create a larger hole for the egg. Place the avocado halves on a baking sheet or in a muffin tin to keep them stable.

3. **Add the eggs:**
   - Crack an egg into each avocado half. If the hole is small, you might use only the yolk and some of the white, or beat the egg first and pour it in. Season with salt and pepper.

4. **Bake:**
   - Place in the oven and bake for about 14-16 minutes, or until the egg whites are set and the yolks are cooked to your liking.

5. **Garnish and serve:**
   - Remove from the oven, sprinkle with chopped chives, cheese, and red pepper flakes if using. Serve immediately.

Bacon-Wrapped Avocado

Yield:
4 servings

Prep Time:
10 minutes

Cook Time:
15 minutes

Total Time:
25 minutes

Nutritional Information
(per serving, approximately):

🔥 **Calories: 320**

Fat: 27g
Protein: 8g
Carbohydrates: 9g
(Net carbs: 4g)
Fiber: 5g

Ingredients:

2 ripe avocados

8 slices of bacon

1/4 teaspoon garlic powder

1/4 teaspoon chili powder

Salt and pepper, to taste

1. **Preheat the oven to 400°F (200°C).**

2. **Prepare the avocados:**
   - Cut the avocados in half and remove the pits. Peel off the skin and then cut each half into two quarters to make eight wedges in total.

3. **Season the avocados:**
   - Sprinkle the avocado wedges with garlic powder, chili powder, salt, and pepper.

4. **Wrap the bacon:**
   - Wrap each avocado wedge with a slice of bacon. You can secure the bacon with a toothpick if necessary.

5. **Bake:**
   - Arrange the bacon-wrapped avocado wedges on a baking sheet lined with parchment paper. Place in the oven and bake for 12-15 minutes or until the bacon is crispy and golden.

6. **Serve:**
   - Allow to cool for a few minutes before serving. These can be enjoyed hot or at room temperature.

Pumpkin Spice Keto Porridge

Yield:
2 servings

Prep Time:
5 minutes

Cook Time:
10 minutes

Total Time:
15 minutes

Nutritional Information
(per serving, approximately):

🔥 **Calories: 280**

Fat: 18g
Protein: 9g
Carbohydrates: 24g
(Net carbs: 8g)
Fiber: 16g

Ingredients:

1/2 cup pumpkin puree (ensure it's unsweetened)

1 cup almond milk (or any keto-friendly milk)

1/4 cup ground flaxseed

1/4 cup chia seeds

2 tablespoons coconut flour

1 tablespoon erythritol or other keto-friendly sweetener

1/2 teaspoon vanilla extract

1 teaspoon pumpkin pie spice

Pinch of salt

Optional toppings: chopped nuts, whipped cream, a sprinkle of cinnamon

1. **Combine ingredients:**
   - In a small pot, mix together the pumpkin puree, almond milk, flaxseed, chia seeds, coconut flour, erythritol, vanilla extract, pumpkin pie spice, and a pinch of salt. Stir well to combine.

2. **Cook the porridge:**
   - Place the pot over medium heat and bring the mixture to a simmer. Reduce the heat to low and cook, stirring frequently, for about 5-8 minutes or until the porridge has thickened to your liking.

3. **Adjust consistency:**
   - If the porridge is too thick, add a little more almond milk until you reach the desired consistency. If it's too thin, cook for a few additional minutes.

4. **Serve:**
   - Divide the porridge into bowls and add any optional toppings like chopped nuts, whipped cream, or a sprinkle of cinnamon.

Zucchini and Herb Breakfast Muffins

Yield:
12 muffins

Prep Time:
15 minutes

Cook Time:
20 minutes

Total Time:
35 minutes

Nutritional Information
(per muffin, approximately):

🔥 Calories: 140

Fat: 10g
Protein: 5g
Carbohydrates: 8g
(Net carbs: 4g)
Fiber: 4g

Ingredients:

2 cups grated zucchini (about 2 medium zucchinis)

1 cup almond flour

1/2 cup coconut flour

1/4 cup grated Parmesan cheese

4 large eggs

1/4 cup olive oil

2 tablespoons fresh chopped herbs (such as parsley, chives, or dill)

1 teaspoon baking powder

1/2 teaspoon garlic powder

Salt and pepper to taste

1. Preheat the oven:

- Preheat the oven to 350°F (175°C). Grease or line a muffin tin with paper liners.

2. Prepare the zucchini:

- After grating the zucchini, wrap it in a clean kitchen towel and squeeze out as much excess moisture as possible.

3. Mix dry ingredients:

- In a large bowl, combine the almond flour, coconut flour, grated Parmesan, baking powder, garlic powder, salt, and pepper.

4. Combine wet ingredients:

- In another bowl, whisk together the eggs and olive oil. Stir in the dried zucchini and chopped herbs.

5. Combine mixtures:

- Add the wet ingredients to the dry ingredients and stir until just combined.

6. Bake:

- Spoon the batter into the prepared muffin tin, filling each cup about three-quarters full. Bake in the preheated oven for 20-25 minutes, or until the tops are golden and a toothpick inserted into the center of a muffin comes out clean.

7. Cool and serve:

- Let the muffins cool in the pan for 5 minutes, then transfer to a wire rack to cool completely.

Cream Cheese Pancakes

Yield:
8 pancakes

Prep Time:
5 minutes

Cook Time:
10 minutes

Total Time:
15 minutes

Nutritional Information
(per pancake, approximately):

🔥 Calories: 110

Fat: 9g
Protein: 4g
Carbohydrates: 2g
(Net carbs: 1g)
Fiber: 1g

Ingredients:
4 ounces cream cheese, softened
4 large eggs
2 tablespoons coconut flour
1 tablespoon erythritol (or other keto-friendly sweetener)
1/2 teaspoon vanilla extract
1/2 teaspoon baking powder
Butter or oil for frying

1. **Prepare the batter:**
   - In a blender or food processor, combine the cream cheese, eggs, coconut flour, erythritol, vanilla extract, and baking powder. Blend until smooth.

2. **Heat the skillet:**
   - Heat a non-stick skillet or griddle over medium heat. Add a little butter or oil to coat the surface.

3. **Cook the pancakes:**
   - Pour or scoop about 1/4 cup of the batter onto the hot skillet for each pancake. Cook for about 2-3 minutes on one side, until bubbles form on the surface and the edges look set. Flip carefully and cook for another 1-2 minutes on the other side until golden brown and cooked through.

4. **Serve:**
   - Serve hot with your favorite keto-friendly syrup or toppings, such as fresh berries or whipped cream.

Ham and Cheese Keto Breakfast Roll-Ups

Yield:
6 roll-ups

Prep Time:
5 minutes

Cook Time:
10 minutes

Total Time:
15 minutes

Nutritional Information
(per roll-up, approximately):

♦ Calories: 200

Fat: 14g
Protein: 17g
Carbohydrates: 1g
(Net carbs: 1g)
Fiber: 0g

Ingredients:

6 large eggs

6 slices of ham (preferably thin and wide slices)

6 slices of cheese (cheddar, Swiss, or your preferred keto-friendly cheese)

Salt and pepper to taste

Optional: herbs like chives or parsley for garnish

1. **Prepare the eggs:**
   - Beat the eggs in a bowl and season with salt and pepper. Heat a non-stick skillet over medium heat and lightly grease it with butter or oil.

2. **Cook the egg crepes:**
   - Pour a thin layer of the beaten eggs into the skillet, tilting to spread evenly and create a thin crepe. Cook for about 1-2 minutes until set, then carefully flip to cook the other side for about 30 seconds. Remove and set aside. Repeat this process for each roll-up.

3. **Assemble the roll-ups:**
   - Lay a slice of ham on each egg crepe, then top with a slice of cheese. Roll up tightly starting from one edge.

4. **Warm the roll-ups:**
   - Place the roll-ups back in the skillet, seam side down, and cook for another 1-2 minutes on each side, or until the cheese is melted and the ham is slightly crispy.

5. **Serve:**
   - Garnish with chopped herbs if desired and serve warm.

Smoked Salmon and Cream Cheese Roll-Ups

Yield:
12 roll-ups

Prep Time:
15 minutes

Cook Time:
0 minutes

Total Time:
15 minutes

Nutritional Information
(per roll-up, approximately):

🔥 **Calories: 60**

Fat: 5g
Protein: 4g
Carbohydrates: 1g
(Net carbs: 1g)
Fiber: 0g

Ingredients:

8 ounces smoked salmon, thinly sliced

4 ounces cream cheese, softened

1 tablespoon capers, drained

2 tablespoons chopped fresh dill

1 tablespoon lemon juice

1/4 teaspoon black pepper

Optional: 1/4 cup thinly sliced red onion or chives for added flavor and crunch

1. **Prepare the filling:**
   - In a small bowl, combine the cream cheese, capers, dill, lemon juice, and black pepper. Mix until smooth and well combined.

2. **Assemble the roll-ups:**
   - Lay out the slices of smoked salmon on a flat surface. Spread a thin layer of the cream cheese mixture over each slice of salmon. If using, add a few slices of red onion or sprinkle some chives across the salmon.

3. **Roll them up:**
   - Carefully roll up each slice of salmon tightly. Place the roll-ups seam side down on a plate.

4. **Chill and serve:**
   - Chill the roll-ups in the refrigerator for about 10 minutes to firm up, which makes them easier to slice. Cut each roll into bite-sized pieces if desired, and serve.

Garlic Butter Mushrooms with Poached Eggs

Yield:
2 servings

Prep Time:
10 minutes

Cook Time:
15 minutes

Total Time:
25 minutes

Nutritional Information
(per serving, approximately):

🔥 Calories: 300

Fat: 23g
Protein: 19g
Carbohydrates: 6g
(Net carbs: 4g)
Fiber: 2g

Ingredients:

8 ounces mushrooms, sliced (such as cremini or button mushrooms)

4 large eggs

3 tablespoons butter

2 cloves garlic, minced

1 tablespoon fresh parsley, chopped

Salt and pepper to taste

Optional: 1 tablespoon white vinegar (for poaching eggs)

1. **Cook the mushrooms:**

- In a large skillet, melt the butter over medium heat. Add the minced garlic and sauté for about 1 minute until fragrant. Add the sliced mushrooms, salt, and pepper. Cook, stirring occasionally, until the mushrooms are golden brown and tender, about 7-10 minutes. Stir in the chopped parsley and remove from heat.

2. **Poach the eggs:**

- While the mushrooms are cooking, bring a pot of water to a gentle simmer. Add a tablespoon of white vinegar if using (this helps the egg whites coagulate). Crack each egg into a small cup or bowl, then gently slide into the simmering water. Cook for about 3-4 minutes for soft poached eggs, or until the whites are firm and the yolks are still runny. Remove the eggs with a slotted spoon and drain on a kitchen towel.

3. **Serve:**

- Divide the sautéed mushrooms between two plates, and top each serving with two poached eggs. Season with additional salt and pepper if desired.

Blueberry Muffins

Yield:
12 muffins

Prep Time:
10 minutes

Cook Time:
20 minutes

Total Time:
30 minutes

Nutritional Information
(per muffin, approximately):

🔥 **Calories: 180**

Fat: 15g
Protein: 5g
Carbohydrates: 6g
(Net carbs: 3g)
Fiber: 3g

Ingredients:

2 cups almond flour

1/3 cup erythritol (or other keto-friendly sweetener)

1 teaspoon baking powder

1/2 teaspoon salt

1/3 cup unsalted butter, melted

3 large eggs

1/3 cup unsweetened almond milk

1 teaspoon vanilla extract

1 cup fresh blueberries (if using frozen, do not thaw)

1. **Preheat the oven:**
   - Preheat the oven to 350°F (175°C). Line a muffin tin with paper liners or grease with butter or non-stick spray.

2. **Mix dry ingredients:**
   - In a large bowl, whisk together the almond flour, erythritol, baking powder, and salt.

3. **Add wet ingredients:**
   - In another bowl, mix the melted butter, eggs, almond milk, and vanilla extract. Stir the wet ingredients into the dry ingredients until just combined.

4. **Fold in the blueberries:**
   - Gently fold the blueberries into the batter, being careful not to crush them.

5. **Fill the muffin cups:**
   - Divide the batter evenly among the prepared muffin cups, filling each about three-quarters full.

6. **Bake:**
   - Place in the oven and bake for 20-25 minutes, or until a toothpick inserted into the center of a muffin comes out clean.

7. **Cool:**
   - Let the muffins cool in the pan for about 5 minutes, then transfer to a wire rack to cool completely.

Spicy Sausage and Kale Breakfast Skillet

Yield:
4 servings

Prep Time:
10 minutes

Cook Time:
20 minutes

Total Time:
30 minutes

Nutritional Information
(per serving, approximately):

🔥 **Calories: 400**

Fat: 30g
Protein: 24g
Carbohydrates: 8g
(Net carbs: 6g)
Fiber: 2g

Ingredients:

1 pound spicy Italian sausage (remove casing if using links)

2 cups chopped kale, stems removed

1 medium onion, diced

1 red bell pepper, diced

4 large eggs

2 cloves garlic, minced

1/4 teaspoon red pepper flakes (adjust to taste)

Salt and pepper to taste

2 tablespoons olive oil

1. **Cook the sausage:**
   - In a large skillet over medium heat, add the sausage. Break it apart with a spoon and cook until browned and no longer pink, about 5-7 minutes. Remove sausage from the skillet and set aside.

2. **Sauté vegetables:**
   - In the same skillet, add the olive oil, diced onion, and bell pepper. Sauté for about 5 minutes until the vegetables start to soften. Add the minced garlic and red pepper flakes, and cook for another minute until fragrant.

3. **Add kale:**
   - Stir in the chopped kale and cook until it begins to wilt, about 3-4 minutes. Season with salt and pepper.

4. **Combine sausage and vegetables:**
   - Return the cooked sausage to the skillet and mix well with the vegetables.

5. **Make space for eggs:**
   - Make four wells in the mixture and crack an egg into each well.

6. **Cook the eggs:**
   - Cover the skillet and cook over medium-low heat for 5-10 minutes, or until the eggs are cooked to your desired doneness.

7. **Serve:**
   - Adjust seasoning if needed and serve hot directly from the skillet.

Lemon Poppy Seed Muffins

Yield:
12 muffins

Prep Time:
15 minutes

Cook Time:
20 minutes

Total Time:
35 minutes

Nutritional Information
(per muffin, approximately):

🔥 **Calories: 190**

Fat: 16g
Protein: 6g
Carbohydrates: 7g
(Net carbs: 3g)
Fiber: 4g

Ingredients:

2 cups almond flour

1/2 cup erythritol (or other keto-friendly sweetener)

1/3 cup coconut flour

2 tablespoons poppy seeds

1 teaspoon baking powder

1/2 teaspoon salt

1/3 cup unsalted butter, melted

4 large eggs

1/2 cup unsweetened almond milk

1/4 cup fresh lemon juice

Zest of 2 lemons

1 teaspoon vanilla extract

1. **Preheat the oven:**
   - Preheat the oven to 350°F (175°C). Line a muffin tin with paper liners or grease with butter or non-stick spray.

2. **Mix dry ingredients:**
   - In a large bowl, combine the almond flour, erythritol, coconut flour, poppy seeds, baking powder, and salt.

3. **Combine wet ingredients:**
   - In another bowl, mix the melted butter, eggs, almond milk, lemon juice, lemon zest, and vanilla extract.

4. **Combine mixtures:**
   - Add the wet ingredients to the dry ingredients and stir until just combined. Be careful not to overmix.

5. **Fill the muffin cups:**
   - Divide the batter evenly among the prepared muffin cups, filling each about three-quarters full.

6. **Bake:**
   - Place in the oven and bake for 20-25 minutes, or until a toothpick inserted into the center of a muffin comes out clean.

7. **Cool:**
   - Let the muffins cool in the pan for about 5 minutes, then transfer to a wire rack to cool completely.

Granola Bars

Yield:
12 bars

Prep Time:
10 minutes

Cook Time:
20 minutes

Total Time:
30 minutes

Nutritional Information
(per bar, approximately):

🔥 **Calories: 270**

Fat: 23g
Protein: 7g
Carbohydrates: 10g
(Net carbs: 4g)
Fiber: 6g

Ingredients:

1 cup almonds, roughly chopped
1 cup pecans, roughly chopped
1/2 cup sunflower seeds
1/2 cup pumpkin seeds
1/4 cup unsweetened shredded coconut
1/4 cup chia seeds
1/4 cup flaxseed meal

1/3 cup butter, melted
1/4 cup almond butter
1/3 cup erythritol (or other keto-friendly sweetener)
1 teaspoon vanilla extract
1/2 teaspoon cinnamon
1/4 teaspoon salt

1. **Preheat the oven:**
   - Preheat the oven to 350°F (175°C). Line a 9x9-inch baking pan with parchment paper, allowing some to overhang for easy removal.

2. **Mix dry ingredients:**
   - In a large bowl, combine the chopped almonds, pecans, sunflower seeds, pumpkin seeds, shredded coconut, chia seeds, and flaxseed meal.

3. **Combine wet ingredients:**
   - In a separate small bowl, mix the melted butter, almond butter, erythritol, vanilla extract, cinnamon, and salt.

4. **Combine mixtures:**
   - Pour the wet ingredients over the dry ingredients and mix well until everything is evenly coated.

5. **Press into pan:**
   - Transfer the mixture to the prepared baking pan and press down firmly to form an even layer.

6. **Bake:**
   - Bake in the preheated oven for about 18-20 minutes, or until the edges are golden brown.

7. **Cool and slice:**
   - Let the granola bars cool in the pan on a wire rack for about 1 hour. Lift the bars out of the pan using the overhanging parchment and slice into 12 bars.

Breakfast Pizza

Yield:
4 servings

Prep Time:
15 minutes

Cook Time:
20 minutes

Total Time:
35 minutes

Nutritional Information
(per serving, approximately):

🔥 Calories: 500

Fat: 40g
Protein: 28g
Carbohydrates: 6g
(Net carbs: 4g)
Fiber: 2g

Ingredients:

For the crust:

1 and 1/2 cups shredded mozzarella cheese

2 tablespoons cream cheese

3/4 cup almond flour

1 large egg

Toppings:

4 eggs

6 slices of bacon, cooked and crumbled

1/2 cup shredded cheddar cheese

1/4 cup finely chopped bell pepper

2 tablespoons chopped green onions

Salt and pepper to taste

1. **Make the dough:**
   - Preheat the oven to 400°F (200°C). In a microwave-safe bowl, combine the mozzarella and cream cheese. Microwave for about 1 minute until the cheeses are melted and can be stirred together. Add the almond flour and an egg to the melted cheese mixture. Mix until a dough forms.
   - Place the dough between two pieces of parchment paper and roll out into a circular pizza shape. Remove the top parchment and transfer the bottom sheet with the dough onto a baking sheet.

2. **Pre-bake the crust:**
   - Poke a few holes in the crust with a fork to prevent bubbling. Bake in the preheated oven for 6-8 minutes until slightly golden. Remove from oven.

3. **Add toppings:**
   - Crack the eggs onto the crust, spacing them out. Sprinkle the crumbled bacon, cheddar cheese, bell pepper, and green onions around the eggs. Season with salt and pepper.

4. **Bake:**
   - Return the pizza to the oven and bake for another 12-15 minutes until the egg whites are set and the crust is golden brown.

5. **Serve:**
   - Cut into slices and serve hot.

Monte Cristo Sandwich

Yield:
2 sandwiches

Prep Time:
15 minutes

Cook Time:
10 minutes

Total Time:
25 minutes

Nutritional Information
(per sandwich, approximately):

🔥 **Calories: 700**

Fat: 56g
Protein: 38g
Carbohydrates: 12g
(Net carbs: 6g)
Fiber: 6g

Ingredients:

For the keto bread:

1/2 cup almond flour

2 tablespoons coconut flour

1 teaspoon baking powder

2 large eggs

2 tablespoons unsalted butter, melted

For the filling:

4 slices Swiss cheese

4 slices deli ham

4 slices deli turkey

For the egg dip:

1 large egg

1/4 cup heavy cream

A pinch of salt

To serve:

Sugar-free raspberry or strawberry jam

Powdered erythritol (optional, for dusting)

1. **Make the keto bread:**
   - In a microwave-safe bowl, mix the almond flour, coconut flour, and baking powder. Stir in the eggs and melted butter until well combined. Divide the mixture into two, and spread into a square or rectangle shape on a parchment-lined microwave-safe plate. Microwave on high for about 90 seconds until firm. Let cool slightly, then slice each piece horizontally to make four slices total.

2. **Prepare the sandwich:**
   - Layer one slice of bread with one slice of Swiss cheese, followed by two slices each of ham and turkey, and another slice of cheese. Top with another slice of bread. Repeat for the second sandwich.

3. **Dip the sandwich:**
   - In a shallow dish, beat the egg with the heavy cream and salt. Dip each sandwich in the egg mixture, coating well on both sides.

4. **Cook the sandwich:**
   - Heat a non-stick skillet over medium heat. Add a bit of butter or oil. Place the dipped sandwiches in the skillet, and cook until golden brown on both sides and the cheese has melted, about 3-4 minutes per side.

5. **Serve:**
   - Slice the sandwiches in half and serve warm with a side of sugar-free jam. Optionally, dust with powdered erythritol for a sweet finish.

Cinnamon Rolls

Yield:
8 cinnamon rolls

Prep Time:
30 minutes

Cook Time:
20 minutes

Total Time:
50 minutes

Nutritional Information
(per cinnamon roll, approximately):

🔥 **Calories: 320**

Fat: 27g
Protein: 11g
Carbohydrates: 6g
(Net carbs: 3g)
Fiber: 3g

Ingredients:

For the dough:
2 cups mozzarella cheese, shredded
2 ounces cream cheese
1 1/2 cups almond flour
2 tablespoons erythritol
1 tablespoon baking powder
1 large egg

For the filling:
1/4 cup butter, softened
2 tablespoons ground cinnamon
1/4 cup erythritol

For the frosting:
4 ounces cream cheese, softened
2 tablespoons butter, softened
1/4 cup powdered erythritol
1/2 teaspoon vanilla extract
1 to 2 tablespoons heavy cream (adjust for desired consistency)

1. **Prepare the dough:**
   - Preheat the oven to 375°F (190°C). In a microwave-safe bowl, combine the mozzarella and cream cheese. Microwave for about 90 seconds, stirring halfway through until completely melted.
   - Stir in the almond flour, erythritol, and baking powder. Add the egg and mix until a dough forms. Roll the dough between two pieces of parchment paper into a rectangular shape.

2. **Add the filling:**
   - Mix the softened butter with cinnamon and erythritol. Spread this mixture evenly over the rolled-out dough.

3. **Roll and cut the dough:**
   - Carefully roll the dough into a log, starting from the long edge. Slice the log into 8 equal pieces and place each piece in a greased baking pan.

4. **Bake:**
   - Bake in the preheated oven for about 20 minutes, or until they are golden and cooked through.

5. **Prepare the frosting:**
   - While the rolls are baking, beat together cream cheese, butter, powdered erythritol, and vanilla extract. Gradually add heavy cream until the frosting reaches a smooth and spreadable consistency.

6. **Frost the rolls:**
   - Once the cinnamon rolls are done, let them cool slightly before spreading the frosting over them.

Stuffed Breakfast Peppers

Yield:
4 servings

Prep Time:
15 minutes

Cook Time:
25 minutes

Total Time:
40 minutes

Nutritional Information
(per serving, approximately):

🔥 **Calories: 400**

Fat: 28g
Protein: 24g
Carbohydrates: 12g
(Net carbs: 9g)
Fiber: 3g

Ingredients:

4 large bell peppers, any color
8 ounces ground sausage
1/2 cup chopped onions
1/2 cup chopped mushrooms
4 large eggs

1/2 cup shredded cheddar cheese
1 tablespoon olive oil
Salt and pepper to taste
Optional: 1/4 teaspoon red pepper flakes for added heat

1. **Preheat the oven:**
   - Preheat your oven to 375°F (190°C).

2. **Prepare the peppers:**
   - Slice the tops off the bell peppers and remove the seeds and membranes. If they don't stand upright, slice a small portion off the bottom to level them. Set aside.

3. **Cook the sausage mixture:**
   - Heat the olive oil in a skillet over medium heat. Add the sausage, breaking it into small pieces with a spatula as it cooks.
   - Once the sausage starts to brown, add the onions and mushrooms. Cook until the vegetables are soft and the sausage is thoroughly cooked. Season with salt, pepper, and red pepper flakes if using.

4. **Assemble the peppers:**
   - Spoon the sausage mixture into the hollowed-out peppers, filling them about halfway.
   - Crack an egg on top of the sausage mixture in each pepper, then sprinkle with shredded cheese.

5. **Bake:**
   - Arrange the stuffed peppers in a baking dish. Bake in the preheated oven for about 20-25 minutes, or until the eggs are set and the cheese is melted and bubbly.

6. **Serve:**
   - Serve the stuffed peppers hot, optionally garnished with fresh herbs like parsley or chives.

Sesame Almond Zoodle Bowl

Yield:
2 servings

Prep Time:
10 minutes

Cook Time:
5 minutes

Total Time:
15 minutes

Nutritional Information
(per serving, approximately):

🔥 **Calories: 300**

Fat: 25g
Protein: 8g
Carbohydrates: 12g
(Net carbs: 8g)
Fiber: 4g

Ingredients:

2 medium zucchinis, spiralized into noodles

1/2 cup sliced almonds, toasted

2 tablespoons sesame oil

1 tablespoon soy sauce (or coconut aminos for a soy-free version)

1 tablespoon rice vinegar

1 clove garlic, minced

1 teaspoon fresh ginger, grated

1 tablespoon sesame seeds

1/4 cup chopped green onions

1/2 teaspoon red pepper flakes (optional for heat)

Salt to taste

1. **Prepare the zoodle base:**
   - In a large bowl, place the spiralized zucchini. Set aside.

2. **Make the dressing:**
   - In a small bowl, whisk together sesame oil, soy sauce (or coconut aminos), rice vinegar, minced garlic, and grated ginger. Adjust seasoning with salt if necessary.

3. **Combine and sauté:**
   - Heat a large skillet over medium heat. Add the zucchini noodles and pour the dressing over them. Toss to coat and cook for about 2–3 minutes, just until the zoodles are slightly softened.

4. **Add toppings:**
   - Remove from heat and toss with toasted almonds, sesame seeds, and green onions. If desired, sprinkle red pepper flakes for some heat.

5. **Serve:**
   - Divide the mixture between two bowls and serve immediately.

Low-Carb Smoothie Bowl

 Yield:
Serves 1

 Prep time:
5 minutes

 Cook time:
0 minutes

 Total Time:
5 minutes

Nutritional Information
(per serving, without toppings):

🔥 **Calories: 400**

Fat: 35g | Carbohydrates: 15g (Net Carbs: 8g) | Fiber: 7g | Protein: 6g

Ingredients:
1/2 cup coconut cream (chilled)
1/4 cup frozen raspberries
1/4 cup frozen strawberries
1 tablespoon chia seeds
1/4 avocado

2 tablespoons unsweetened almond milk (adjust for desired consistency)
Sweetener to taste (such as erythritol or stevia)
Optional toppings: hemp seeds, coconut flakes, nuts, or additional berries

1. **Blend the Smoothie:** In a blender, combine the coconut cream, frozen raspberries, frozen strawberries, chia seeds, avocado, and almond milk. Blend until smooth. Add sweetener to your taste and blend again to mix well.

2. **Adjust Consistency:** If the smoothie is too thick, add a little more almond milk and blend until you reach the desired consistency.

3. **Serve:** Pour the smoothie into a bowl. Garnish with your choice of optional toppings like hemp seeds, coconut flakes, nuts, or a few fresh berries.

Peanut Butter Keto Smoothie

 Yield:
2 servings

 Prep time:
5 minutes

 Cook time:
0 minutes

 Total Time:
5 minutes

Nutritional Information
(per serving, approximately):

🔥 **Calories: 300**

Fat: 28g | Protein: 6g | Carbohydrates: 5g (Net carbs: 3g) | Fiber: 2g

Ingredients:
2 tablespoons natural peanut butter (no added sugar)
1 cup unsweetened almond milk
1/4 cup heavy cream

1 tablespoon MCT oil (optional for added fat boost)
1/2 teaspoon vanilla extract
2 tablespoons erythritol (or another keto-friendly sweetener)
Ice cubes (as needed for thickness)

1. **Blend ingredients:** In a blender, combine the peanut butter, almond milk, heavy cream, MCT oil (if using), vanilla extract, erythritol, and ice cubes. Blend on high until smooth and creamy. Adjust the amount of ice to reach your desired consistency.

2. **Taste and adjust:** Taste the smoothie and adjust sweetness or thickness as needed. If it's too thick, add a bit more almond milk. If it needs more sweetness, add a little extra erythritol or sweetener of choice.

3. **Serve:** Pour the smoothie into glasses and serve immediately. You can top with a sprinkle of crushed peanuts or a drizzle of peanut butter for extra flavor.

Smoothie with Avocado and Cocoa

Yield:
2 servings

Prep time:
5 minutes

Cook time:
0 minutes

Total Time:
5 minutes

Nutritional Information
(per serving, approximately):

Calories: 350

Fat: 32g | Protein: 4g | Carbohydrates: 12g (Net carbs: 4g) | Fiber: 8g

Ingredients:

1 medium avocado, peeled and pitted

2 tablespoons unsweetened cocoa powder

1 cup unsweetened almond milk

1/2 cup heavy cream

2 tablespoons erythritol (or other keto-friendly sweetener)

1 teaspoon vanilla extract

Ice cubes (adjust quantity for desired thickness)

Optional: a pinch of salt to enhance flavors

1. **Blend the ingredients:** In a blender, combine the avocado, cocoa powder, almond milk, heavy cream, erythritol, vanilla extract, and a handful of ice cubes. Add a pinch of salt if desired. Blend on high until smooth and creamy.

2. **Adjust consistency:** If the smoothie is too thick, add more almond milk to reach your desired consistency. Blend again briefly.

3. **Serve:** Pour the smoothie into glasses and serve immediately. You can top with a sprinkle of cocoa powder or some keto-friendly whipped cream for an extra treat.

Cottage Cheese Bowls

Yield:
2 servings

Prep time:
5 minutes

Cook time:
0 minutes

Total Time:
5 minutes

Nutritional Information
(per serving, approximately):

Calories: 220

Fat: 15g | Protein: 14g | Carbohydrates: 8g (Net carbs: 5g) | Fiber: 3g

Ingredients:

1 cup full-fat cottage cheese

1/4 cup chopped nuts (such as almonds, walnuts, or pecans)

1/4 cup fresh berries (like raspberries or blueberries; ensure to adjust for keto-friendly portions)

1 tablespoon chia seeds

1/2 teaspoon vanilla extract

Sweetener to taste (such as stevia or erythritol)

A pinch of cinnamon (optional)

1. **Prepare the cottage cheese:** In a mixing bowl, combine the cottage cheese with vanilla extract, sweetener, and a pinch of cinnamon if using. Mix well until everything is evenly incorporated.

2. **Assemble the bowls:** Divide the cottage cheese mixture into two serving bowls.

3. **Add toppings:** Sprinkle each bowl with chopped nuts, fresh berries, and chia seeds.

4. **Serve:** Enjoy immediately for a fresh and filling breakfast or snack.

CHAPTER 3

Poultry

Chicken Parmesan

Yield:
4 servings

Prep Time:
15 minutes

Cook Time:
25 minutes

Total Time:
40 minutes

Nutritional Information
(per serving):

🔥 **Calories: 495**

Protein: 42 g
Fat: 31 g
Carbohydrates: 8 g
Fiber: 3 g
Net Carbs: 5 g

Ingredients:

4 boneless, skinless chicken breasts
Salt and pepper, to taste
1 cup almond flour
2 large eggs, beaten
1 cup grated Parmesan cheese
1 teaspoon garlic powder

1 teaspoon Italian seasoning
1 cup marinara sauce (sugar-free)
1 cup shredded mozzarella cheese
2 tablespoons olive oil
Fresh basil leaves, for garnish

1. **Prepare Chicken:**
   - Preheat your oven to 375ºF (190ºC). Pound the chicken breasts to an even thickness, about 1/2 inch, then season both sides with salt and pepper.

2. **Coat the Chicken:**
   - In one shallow dish, place the beaten eggs. In another shallow dish, mix the almond flour, Parmesan cheese, garlic powder, and Italian seasoning. Dip each chicken breast first into the egg, then dredge in the almond flour mixture, pressing to coat.

3. **Cook Chicken:**
   - Heat the olive oil in a large oven-safe skillet over medium-high heat. Add the chicken and cook until each side is golden brown, about 3-4 minutes per side.

4. **Add Sauce and Cheese:**
   - Pour the marinara sauce over the chicken in the skillet. Sprinkle the shredded mozzarella cheese evenly over the top.

5. **Bake:**
   - Transfer the skillet to the oven and bake for about 15-20 minutes, or until the chicken is cooked through and the cheese is bubbly and slightly golden.

6. **Garnish and Serve:**
   - Garnish with fresh basil leaves before serving.

Buffalo Chicken Stuffed Peppers

Yield:
4 servings

Prep Time:
20 minutes

Cook Time:
20 minutes

Total Time:
40 minutes

Nutritional Information
(per serving):

🔥 **Calories: 330**

Protein: 23 g
Fat: 23 g
Carbohydrates: 8 g
Fiber: 2 g
Net Carbs: 6 g

Ingredients:

4 large bell peppers (any color), tops cut off and seeds removed

2 cups cooked chicken, shredded

1/2 cup buffalo sauce

1/4 cup cream cheese, softened

1/4 cup ranch dressing

1/2 cup shredded cheddar cheese

1/4 cup green onions, chopped

Salt and pepper, to taste

Optional: extra ranch or blue cheese dressing for drizzling

1. **Preheat Oven:**
   - Preheat your oven to 375°F (190°C).

2. **Prepare Peppers:**
   - Arrange the bell peppers in a baking dish, cut-side up. Lightly season the insides with salt and pepper.

3. **Mix Filling:**
   - In a large bowl, combine the shredded chicken with buffalo sauce, cream cheese, and ranch dressing. Mix until everything is well incorporated.

4. **Stuff Peppers:**
   - Spoon the buffalo chicken mixture into each bell pepper. Top each with shredded cheddar cheese.

5. **Bake:**
   - Place the stuffed peppers in the preheated oven and bake for 20 minutes, or until the peppers are tender and the cheese is melted and bubbly.

6. **Garnish and Serve:**
   - Sprinkle chopped green onions over the top. Serve hot, with extra ranch or blue cheese dressing drizzled on top if desired.

Creamy Tuscan Garlic Chicken

Yield:
4 servings

Prep Time:
10 minutes

Cook Time:
20 minutes

Total Time:
30 minutes

Nutritional Information
(per serving):

🔥 **Calories: 490**

Protein: 31 g
Fat: 37 g
Carbohydrates: 7 g
Fiber: 1 g
Net Carbs: 6 g

Ingredients:

4 boneless, skinless chicken breasts

Salt and pepper, to taste

2 tablespoons olive oil

3 cloves garlic, minced

1 cup heavy cream

1/2 cup chicken broth

1/2 cup grated Parmesan cheese

1 teaspoon Italian seasoning

1/2 cup sun-dried tomatoes, chopped

2 cups fresh spinach

Additional grated Parmesan cheese for garnish

1. **Prepare Chicken:**
   • Season the chicken breasts generously with salt and pepper.

2. **Cook Chicken:**
   • In a large skillet, heat olive oil over medium-high heat. Add the chicken breasts and cook until golden on both sides and cooked through, about 6-8 minutes per side depending on thickness. Remove chicken from the skillet and set aside.

3. **Make the Sauce:**
   • In the same skillet, add minced garlic and sauté for about 1 minute until fragrant. Pour in the heavy cream, chicken broth, and Parmesan cheese. Bring to a simmer, then add Italian seasoning and sun-dried tomatoes. Let the sauce simmer for about 5 minutes to thicken slightly.

4. **Add Spinach:**
   • Stir in the spinach and continue to simmer until the spinach wilts, about 2-3 minutes. Adjust seasoning with salt and pepper to taste.

5. **Combine:**
   • Return the cooked chicken to the skillet and spoon the sauce over the chicken. Cook for an additional 2-3 minutes to reheat the chicken.

6. **Serve:**
   • Garnish with additional grated Parmesan cheese and serve hot.

Spinach and Feta Stuffed Chicken

Yield:
4 servings

Prep Time:
15 minutes

Cook Time:
25 minutes

Total Time:
40 minutes

Nutritional Information
(per serving):

🔥 **Calories: 290**

Protein: 31 g
Fat: 17 g
Carbohydrates: 2 g
Fiber: 0.5 g
Net Carbs: 1.5 g

Ingredients:

4 boneless, skinless chicken breasts

Salt and pepper, to taste

2 tablespoons olive oil

1 cup fresh spinach, chopped

1/2 cup feta cheese, crumbled

1 teaspoon garlic powder

1/2 teaspoon dried oregano

1/2 teaspoon red pepper flakes (optional)

Toothpicks or kitchen twine for securing

1. **Preheat Oven:**
   - Preheat your oven to 375°F (190°C).

2. **Prepare Chicken:**
   - Place each chicken breast between two pieces of plastic wrap and pound with a meat mallet or rolling pin until about 1/4 inch thick. Season both sides with salt and pepper.

3. **Make Filling:**
   - In a small bowl, mix together the chopped spinach, crumbled feta, garlic powder, oregano, and red pepper flakes.

4. **Stuff Chicken:**
   - Divide the spinach and feta mixture evenly among the chicken breasts. Roll up each breast tightly and secure with toothpicks or tie with kitchen twine.

5. **Cook Chicken:**
   - Heat olive oil in a large oven-safe skillet over medium-high heat. Add the stuffed chicken and sear until golden brown on all sides, about 3-4 minutes per side.

6. **Bake:**
   - Transfer the skillet to the preheated oven and bake the chicken for 15-20 minutes, or until the chicken is cooked through and reaches an internal temperature of 165°F (74°C).

7. **Serve:**
   - Remove the toothpicks or twine before serving. Optionally, drizzle with a little olive oil or a squeeze of lemon for added flavor.

Chicken Salad

Yield:
4 servings

Prep Time:
15 minutes

Cook Time:
0 minutes
(assuming pre-cooked chicken)

Total Time:
15 minutes

Nutritional Information
(per serving):

🔥 **Calories: 280**

Protein: 18 g
Fat: 22 g
Carbohydrates: 3 g
Fiber: 1 g
Net Carbs: 2 g

Ingredients:

2 cups cooked chicken, shredded or chopped

1/2 cup celery, diced

1/4 cup red onion, finely chopped

1/4 cup pecans, chopped

1/4 cup mayonnaise

2 tablespoons sour cream

1 tablespoon Dijon mustard

1 tablespoon fresh lemon juice

1 teaspoon dried parsley

Salt and pepper, to taste

Optional: 1/4 teaspoon garlic powder

Optional: 2 tablespoons fresh dill, chopped

1. **Combine Ingredients:**
   - In a large bowl, combine the shredded chicken, celery, red onion, and pecans.

2. **Prepare Dressing:**
   - In a small bowl, whisk together the mayonnaise, sour cream, Dijon mustard, lemon juice, dried parsley, and optional garlic powder. Season with salt and pepper to taste.

3. **Mix Salad:**
   - Pour the dressing over the chicken mixture and toss until everything is evenly coated. If using, stir in the chopped fresh dill.

4. **Chill and Serve:**
   - For the best flavor, let the salad chill in the refrigerator for at least 30 minutes before serving. This allows the flavors to meld together beautifully.

5. **Serving Suggestions:**
   - Serve the chicken salad on a bed of mixed greens, wrapped in lettuce leaves for a low-carb wrap, or enjoy it as is for a quick and satisfying meal.

Lemon Herb Roasted Chicken

Yield:
4 servings

Prep Time:
15 minutes

Cook Time:
1 hour 20 minutes

Total Time:
1 hour 35 minutes

Nutritional Information
(per serving):

♦ Calories: 430

Protein: 35 g
Fat: 30 g
Carbohydrates: 3 g
Fiber: 1 g
Net Carbs: 2 g

Ingredients:

1 whole chicken (about 4 to 5 pounds)

2 tablespoons olive oil

2 lemons, one juiced and one cut into wedges

4 garlic cloves, minced

1 tablespoon fresh rosemary, chopped

1 tablespoon fresh thyme, chopped

1 tablespoon fresh parsley, chopped

Salt and pepper, to taste

1. **Preheat Oven:**
   - Preheat your oven to 425°F (220°C).

2. **Prepare Chicken:**
   - Pat the chicken dry with paper towels. Rub the entire surface of the chicken with olive oil, and then season generously inside and out with salt and pepper.

3. **Season Chicken:**
   - In a small bowl, combine the lemon juice, minced garlic, rosemary, thyme, and parsley. Rub this herb mixture all over the chicken, both under and over the skin.

4. **Stuff Chicken:**
   - Place the lemon wedges and any additional herbs inside the cavity of the chicken.

5. **Roast Chicken:**
   - Place the chicken breast-side up in a roasting pan. Roast in the pre-heated oven for about 20 minutes. Reduce the oven temperature to 350°F (175°C) and continue roasting for about 1 hour, or until the chicken is golden brown and a meat thermometer inserted into the thickest part of the thigh reads 165°F (74°C).

6. **Rest and Serve:**
   - Remove the chicken from the oven and let it rest for 10 minutes before carving. Serve with additional lemon wedges and garnish with fresh herbs.

Chicken Tenders

Yield:
4 servings

Prep Time:
15 minutes

Cook Time:
20 minutes

Total Time:
35 minutes

Nutritional Information
(per serving):

🔥 **Calories: 320**

Protein: 29 g
Fat: 20 g
Carbohydrates: 5 g
Fiber: 2 g
Net Carbs: 3 g

Ingredients:

1 pound chicken tenderloins

1 cup almond flour

1 teaspoon paprika

1/2 teaspoon garlic powder

1/2 teaspoon onion powder

Salt and pepper, to taste

2 large eggs

2 tablespoons heavy cream

Cooking spray or olive oil for greasing

1. **Preheat Oven and Prepare Baking Sheet:**
   - Preheat your oven to 400°F (200°C). Line a baking sheet with parchment paper and lightly grease it with cooking spray or olive oil.

2. **Prepare Egg Wash:**
   - In a shallow dish, whisk together the eggs and heavy cream.

3. **Mix Dry Ingredients:**
   - In another shallow dish, combine the almond flour, paprika, garlic powder, onion powder, salt, and pepper.

4. **Coat Chicken:**
   - Dip each chicken tender first into the egg wash, then dredge in the almond flour mixture, pressing to coat thoroughly. Place the coated tenders on the prepared baking sheet.

5. **Bake:**
   - Bake in the preheated oven for 20 minutes, flipping halfway through, until the chicken is golden brown and cooked through.

6. **Serve:**
   - Serve hot with your favorite keto-friendly dipping sauces, such as ranch dressing or sugar-free barbecue sauce.

Garlic Parmesan Wings

Yield:
4 servings

Prep Time:
10 minutes

Cook Time:
45 minutes

Total Time:
55 minutes

Nutritional Information
(per serving):

🔥 **Calories: 410**

Protein: 25 g
Fat: 34 g
Carbohydrates: 1 g
Fiber: 0 g
Net Carbs: 1 g

Ingredients:

2 pounds chicken wings, tips removed and wings split at the joint

2 tablespoons olive oil

Salt and pepper, to taste

4 cloves garlic, minced

4 tablespoons butter

1/2 cup grated Parmesan cheese

1 teaspoon dried parsley

Optional: Red pepper flakes for a spicy kick

1. **Preheat Oven and Prepare Wings:**
   - Preheat your oven to 400°F (200°C). Pat the wings dry with paper towels to ensure they get crispy. Toss the wings with olive oil, salt, and pepper in a large bowl.

2. **Bake Wings:**
   - Arrange the wings in a single layer on a baking sheet lined with parchment paper. Bake for about 45 minutes, or until the skin is crispy and golden brown, turning once halfway through cooking.

3. **Prepare Garlic Parmesan Sauce:**
   - While the wings are baking, melt the butter in a small saucepan over medium heat. Add the minced garlic and sauté until fragrant, about 1 minute. Remove from heat and stir in the grated Parmesan cheese and dried parsley. If using, add red pepper flakes to taste.

4. **Toss Wings in Sauce:**
   - Remove the wings from the oven and place them in a large bowl. Pour the garlic Parmesan sauce over the wings and toss well to coat evenly.

5. **Serve:**
   - Serve the wings hot, garnished with extra Parmesan cheese or parsley if desired.

Turkey Meatballs

Yield:
4 servings

Prep Time:
15 minutes

Cook Time:
20 minutes

Total Time:
35 minutes

Nutritional Information
(per serving):

🔥 **Calories: 280**

Protein: 28 g
Fat: 18 g
Carbohydrates: 2 g
Fiber: 1 g
Net Carbs: 1 g

Ingredients:

1 pound ground turkey
1/4 cup almond flour
1 large egg
1/4 cup grated Parmesan cheese
2 tablespoons fresh parsley,
chopped
1 teaspoon garlic powder
1 teaspoon onion powder
Salt and pepper, to taste
2 tablespoons olive oil for frying

1. **Mix Ingredients:**
   - In a large bowl, combine the ground turkey, almond flour, egg, grated Parmesan, chopped parsley, garlic powder, onion powder, salt, and pepper. Mix thoroughly until all ingredients are well incorporated.

2. **Form Meatballs:**
   - With clean hands, shape the mixture into small balls, about 1 to 1.5 inches in diameter.

3. **Cook Meatballs:**
   - Heat the olive oil in a large skillet over medium heat. Add the meatballs and cook, turning occasionally, until browned on all sides and cooked through, about 10-12 minutes. Depending on the size of your skillet, you may need to work in batches to avoid overcrowding the pan.

4. **Drain:**
   - Once cooked, transfer the meatballs to a plate lined with paper towels to drain excess oil.

5. **Serve:**
   - Serve the turkey meatballs hot. They can be enjoyed on their own, with a side of keto-friendly marinara sauce, or over zucchini noodles for a complete meal.

Chicken Bacon Ranch Casserole

Yield:
6 servings

Prep Time:
20 minutes

Cook Time:
25 minutes

Total Time:
45 minutes

Nutritional Information
(per serving):

🔥 **Calories: 450**

Protein: 25 g
Fat: 36 g
Carbohydrates: 5 g
Fiber: 1 g
Net Carbs: 4 g

Ingredients:

2 cups cooked chicken, shredded

6 slices bacon, cooked and chopped

1 tablespoon olive oil

1 medium onion, chopped

2 cloves garlic, minced

1 cup heavy cream

1/2 cup cream cheese, softened

1/2 cup chicken broth

1/3 cup ranch dressing

1 cup cheddar cheese, shredded

1/2 teaspoon paprika

Salt and pepper, to taste

1/4 cup green onions, sliced (for garnish)

Optional: 1/2 cup chopped broccoli or spinach for added nutrients

1. **Preheat Oven:**
   - Preheat your oven to 375°F (190°C).

2. **Prepare Vegetables:**
   - In a large skillet, heat olive oil over medium heat. Add the chopped onion and sauté until translucent, about 5 minutes. Add the minced garlic and sauté for another minute until fragrant.

3. **Combine Ingredients:**
   - In a large mixing bowl, combine the cooked chicken, cooked bacon, sautéed onions and garlic, heavy cream, cream cheese, chicken broth, and ranch dressing. Stir until everything is well mixed. If using, fold in the optional broccoli or spinach.

4. **Add Cheese and Season:**
   - Stir in half of the shredded cheddar cheese and season the mixture with paprika, salt, and pepper.

5. **Bake:**
   - Transfer the mixture to a greased baking dish. Top with the remaining cheddar cheese. Bake in the preheated oven for 25 minutes, or until the casserole is bubbly and golden on top.

6. **Garnish and Serve:**
   - Garnish with sliced green onions before serving.

Spinach Artichoke Chicken

Yield:
4 servings

Prep Time:
15 minutes

Cook Time:
25 minutes

Total Time:
40 minutes

Nutritional Information
(per serving):

🔥 **Calories: 450**

Protein: 32 g
Fat: 34 g
Carbohydrates: 6 g
Fiber: 2 g
Net Carbs: 4 g

Ingredients:

4 boneless, skinless chicken breasts

Salt and pepper, to taste

1 tablespoon olive oil

2 cloves garlic, minced

1 cup heavy cream

1/2 cup grated Parmesan cheese

1/2 cup sour cream

1 can (14 ounces) artichoke hearts, drained and chopped

1 cup fresh spinach, chopped

1/2 teaspoon red pepper flakes (optional for heat)

1/2 teaspoon Italian seasoning

1. **Preheat Oven:**
   - Preheat your oven to 375°F (190°C).

2. **Prepare Chicken:**
   - Season chicken breasts with salt and pepper. Heat olive oil in a large oven-safe skillet over medium-high heat. Add the chicken breasts and sear each side until golden brown, about 3-4 minutes per side. Remove chicken from skillet and set aside.

3. **Make Sauce:**
   - In the same skillet, add minced garlic and sauté for 1 minute until fragrant. Reduce heat to low and stir in heavy cream, Parmesan cheese, and sour cream. Cook until the mixture begins to simmer.

4. **Add Vegetables:**
   - Stir in chopped artichoke hearts, spinach, red pepper flakes (if using), and Italian seasoning. Cook for another 2-3 minutes until the spinach starts to wilt.

5. **Combine and Bake:**
   - Return the chicken to the skillet, spooning the sauce and vegetables over the chicken. Place the skillet in the preheated oven and bake for 15-20 minutes, or until the chicken is thoroughly cooked and the sauce is bubbly.

6. **Serve:**
   - Serve hot, ensuring each plate gets a generous helping of the spinach artichoke sauce.

Bacon-Wrapped Chicken Livers

Yield:
4 servings

Prep Time:
15 minutes

Cook Time:
20 minutes

Total Time:
35 minutes

Nutritional Information
(per serving):

🔥 **Calories: 330**

Protein: 22 g
Fat: 25 g
Carbohydrates: 1 g
Fiber: 0 g
Net Carbs: 1 g

Ingredients:

1 pound chicken livers, cleaned and halved

8 slices of bacon, cut in half

Salt and pepper, to taste

Optional: 1/4 teaspoon garlic powder

Optional: 1/4 teaspoon smoked paprika

Toothpicks, for securing

1. **Preheat Oven and Prepare Baking Sheet:**
   - Preheat your oven to 400°F (200°C). Line a baking sheet with parchment paper or aluminum foil for easy cleanup.

2. **Season Chicken Livers:**
   - Season the chicken livers with salt, pepper, garlic powder, and smoked paprika if using.

3. **Wrap with Bacon:**
   - Wrap each chicken liver half with a half slice of bacon, securing it with a toothpick. Make sure the bacon is snug but not too tight.

4. **Arrange on Baking Sheet:**
   - Place the bacon-wrapped livers on the prepared baking sheet, ensuring they do not touch each other.

5. **Bake:**
   - Bake in the preheated oven for about 20 minutes, or until the bacon is crispy and the livers are cooked through.

6. **Broil for Crispiness:**
   - For extra crispiness, broil on high for the last 2-3 minutes, watching carefully to avoid burning.

7. **Serve:**
   - Serve hot, either as an appetizer with keto-friendly dips or as a side dish with your main meal.

Chicken Liver Mousse

Yield:
8 servings

Prep Time:
15 minutes

Cook Time:
10 minutes

Total Time:
25 minutes,
plus chilling

Nutritional Information
(per serving):

🔥 Calories: 200

Protein: 7 g
Fat: 18 g
Carbohydrates: 1 g
Fiber: 0 g
Net Carbs: 1 g

Ingredients:

1 pound chicken livers, cleaned and trimmed

1/2 cup unsalted butter, divided

1 small onion, finely chopped

2 cloves garlic, minced

1/4 cup heavy cream

2 tablespoons brandy or cognac (optional)

1 teaspoon fresh thyme leaves

Salt and pepper, to taste

Additional melted butter for sealing (optional)

1. **Sauté Aromatics:**
   - In a large skillet, melt half of the butter over medium heat. Add the onion and garlic, sautéing until the onion is translucent and softened, about 3-4 minutes.

2. **Cook Livers:**
   - Add the chicken livers to the skillet, cooking until they are browned on the outside but still slightly pink in the center, about 3-5 minutes per side. Do not overcook to avoid a grainy texture.

3. **Deglaze and Simmer:**
   - If using, pour in the brandy or cognac and let it simmer for a minute to cook off the alcohol. Add the thyme, and season with salt and pepper.

4. **Blend Mixture:**
   - Transfer the liver mixture to a food processor. Add the remaining butter and heavy cream. Blend until the mixture is smooth and creamy.

5. **Chill:**
   - Pour the mousse into a serving dish or individual ramekins. For a traditional touch, seal the top with a thin layer of melted butter to prevent oxidation. Chill in the refrigerator for at least 2 hours or until firm.

6. **Serve:**
   - Serve chilled. The mousse pairs beautifully with keto-friendly crackers, cucumber slices, or as a spread on low-carb toast.

Chicken Liver Salad

Yield:
4 servings

Prep Time:
15 minutes

Cook Time:
10 minutes

Total Time:
25 minutes

Nutritional Information
(per serving):

🔥 **Calories: 320**

Protein: 24 g
Fat: 22 g
Carbohydrates: 6 g
Fiber: 2 g
Net Carbs: 4 g

Ingredients:

1 pound chicken livers, cleaned and trimmed

2 tablespoons olive oil

1 tablespoon balsamic vinegar

1 teaspoon Dijon mustard

Salt and pepper, to taste

6 cups mixed salad greens (such as arugula, spinach, and romaine)

1/2 cup cherry tomatoes, halved

1/4 red onion, thinly sliced

1/4 cup chopped walnuts

Optional: 2 hard-boiled eggs, sliced

1. **Cook Chicken Livers:**
   - Heat 1 tablespoon of olive oil in a skillet over medium heat. Add the chicken livers and season with salt and pepper. Cook until the livers are browned on the outside but still slightly pink in the middle, about 3-4 minutes per side. Remove from heat and let them cool slightly.

2. **Prepare Dressing:**
   - In a small bowl, whisk together the remaining olive oil, balsamic vinegar, Dijon mustard, salt, and pepper.

3. **Assemble Salad:**
   - In a large salad bowl, toss the salad greens with cherry tomatoes, red onion, and walnuts. Slice the cooked chicken livers and add them to the salad. If using, add the sliced hard-boiled eggs.

4. **Dress and Serve:**
   - Drizzle the dressing over the salad and gently toss to combine. Serve immediately.

Chicken Liver and Mushroom Bake

Yield:
4 servings

Prep Time:
15 minutes

Cook Time:
30 minutes

Total Time:
45 minutes

Nutritional Information
(per serving):

🔥 **Calories: 350**

Protein: 25 g
Fat: 26 g
Carbohydrates: 5 g
Fiber: 1 g
Net Carbs: 4 g

Ingredients:

1 pound chicken livers, cleaned and trimmed

1 tablespoon olive oil

1 medium onion, finely chopped

2 cloves garlic, minced

2 cups mushrooms, sliced

1/2 cup heavy cream

1/4 cup chicken broth

1 tablespoon Dijon mustard

1/2 teaspoon thyme

Salt and pepper, to taste

1/2 cup grated Parmesan cheese

1. **Preheat Oven:**
   - Preheat your oven to 375°F (190°C).

2. **Prepare Chicken Livers:**
   - Heat olive oil in a large skillet over medium heat. Add chicken livers and cook until browned on all sides, about 5 minutes. Remove from the skillet and set aside.

3. **Cook Vegetables:**
   - In the same skillet, add onion and garlic, and sauté until the onion is translucent. Add mushrooms and continue to cook until the mushrooms are soft and golden, about 5-7 minutes.

4. **Make Sauce:**
   - Stir in heavy cream, chicken broth, Dijon mustard, thyme, salt, and pepper. Bring to a simmer and let cook for a few minutes until slightly thickened.

5. **Combine Ingredients:**
   - Chop the cooked chicken livers into bite-sized pieces and return them to the skillet with the mushroom sauce. Stir well to combine.

6. **Bake:**
   - Transfer the mixture to a greased baking dish. Sprinkle with grated Parmesan cheese. Bake in the preheated oven for 20 minutes or until the top is golden brown and bubbly.

7. **Serve:**
   - Serve hot, ideally with a side of keto-friendly vegetables or a fresh salad.

Turkey Pot Pie

Yield:
Serves 6

Prep Time:
15 minutes

Cook Time:
45 minutes

Total Time:
1 hour

Nutritional Information
(per serving, approximately):

🔥 **Calories:**
400

Fat: 30g
Carbohydrates: 8g net (10g total carbs minus 2g fiber)
Protein: 22g

Ingredients:

For the filling:

2 tablespoons olive oil

1 medium onion, diced

2 cloves garlic, minced

2 cups cooked turkey, chopped

1 cup cauliflower florets, chopped

1/2 cup celery, diced

1/2 cup carrot (optional, can be omitted for stricter keto)

1 cup turkey or chicken broth

1/2 cup heavy cream

Salt and pepper to taste

1 teaspoon dried thyme

1 teaspoon dried parsley

For the crust:

1 1/2 cups almond flour

1/4 cup coconut flour

1/2 teaspoon xanthan gum

1/2 teaspoon salt

1/4 cup unsalted butter, melted

1 large egg

1. **Preheat oven to 375°F (190°C).**

2. **Prepare the filling:**
   - Heat olive oil in a large skillet over medium heat.
   - Add onion and garlic, sauté until onions are translucent.
   - Add cauliflower, celery, and carrot. Cook until vegetables are slightly tender.
   - Stir in the cooked turkey, broth, heavy cream, salt, pepper, thyme, and parsley. Bring to a simmer.
   - Let the mixture cook until slightly thickened, about 10 minutes, then remove from heat.

3. **Prepare the crust:**
   - In a bowl, mix together almond flour, coconut flour, xanthan gum, and salt.
   - Add melted butter and egg, mixing until a dough forms.
   - Roll out the dough between two pieces of parchment paper to the size of your pie dish.

4. **Assemble the pie:**
   - Transfer the filling into a greased pie dish.
   - Place the dough over the top of the filling, pressing down the edges to seal.
   - Make a few slits in the crust to allow steam to escape.

5. **Bake:** Place in the preheated oven and bake for 25–30 minutes, or until the crust is golden brown.

6. **Serve hot.**

Turkey Chili

Yield:
Serves 6

Prep Time:
15 minutes

Cook Time:
30 minutes

Total Time:
45 minutes

Nutritional Information
(per serving,
approximately):

🔥 **Calories: 280**

Fat: 15g
Carbohydrates: 7g net
(9g total carbs minus 2g
fiber)
Protein: 28g

Ingredients:

2 tablespoons olive oil
1 large onion, chopped
3 cloves garlic, minced
1 bell pepper, chopped (any color)
2 pounds ground turkey
1 tablespoon chili powder
1 teaspoon cumin
1/2 teaspoon paprika

1/4 teaspoon cayenne pepper
(adjust to taste)
Salt and black pepper to taste
1 can (14.5 ounces) diced tomatoes,
no added sugar
2 cups beef broth (or chicken broth)
1/2 cup chopped fresh cilantro
(optional for garnishing)

1. **Heat the oil:**
   - In a large pot, heat the olive oil over medium heat. Add the onion, garlic, and bell pepper, cooking until the vegetables are softened, about 5 minutes.

2. **Cook the turkey:**
   - Add the ground turkey to the pot. Break it apart with a spoon and cook until it is no longer pink.

3. **Add spices and liquids:**
   - Stir in the chili powder, cumin, paprika, cayenne, salt, and black pepper. Cook for about 2 minutes until fragrant.
   - Add the diced tomatoes and broth. Stir well to combine.

4. **Simmer:**
   - Reduce heat to low and let the chili simmer, uncovered, for about 20-25 minutes. Stir occasionally.

5. **Final touches:**
   - Taste and adjust seasoning if needed. If the chili is too thick, add more broth to reach your desired consistency.

6. **Serve:**
   - Serve hot, garnished with chopped cilantro if desired.

Turkey Heart Pâté

Yield:
Makes about 2 cups

Prep Time:
15 minutes

Cook Time:
45 minutes

Total Time:
1 hour

Nutritional Information
(per serving, about 2 tablespoons, approximately):

🔥 **Calories: 150**

Fat: 12g
Carbohydrates: 2g net
Protein: 8g

Ingredients:

1 pound turkey hearts, cleaned and trimmed

2 tablespoons butter

1 small onion, finely chopped

2 cloves garlic, minced

1 bay leaf

1 teaspoon thyme

1/4 cup brandy or cognac (optional, can substitute with broth)

1/2 cup heavy cream

Salt and black pepper to taste

2 tablespoons fresh parsley, chopped (for garnish)

1. **Precook the turkey hearts:**
   - In a medium saucepan, cover the turkey hearts with water and add a pinch of salt. Bring to a boil, then reduce the heat and simmer for 20 minutes. Drain and allow to cool slightly.

2. **Sauté the aromatics:**
   - In the same pan, melt the butter over medium heat. Add the chopped onion and garlic, sautéing until they are soft and translucent, about 5-7 minutes.

3. **Cook the turkey hearts with seasonings:**
   - Add the precooked turkey hearts back to the pan along with the bay leaf and thyme. Sauté for another 10 minutes, stirring occasionally.

4. **Deglaze the pan:**
   - Pour in the brandy or cognac (or broth, if substituting) and scrape up any browned bits from the bottom of the pan. Allow the liquid to reduce by half, about 5 minutes.

5. **Blend the mixture:**
   - Remove the bay leaf. Transfer the turkey heart mixture to a food processor, including the cream, and blend until smooth. Season with salt and pepper to taste.

6. **Chill:**
   - Transfer the pâté to a bowl or mold, cover, and refrigerate for at least 2 hours, or until firm.

7. **Serve:**
   - Garnish with fresh parsley before serving. Enjoy with keto-friendly crackers or sliced vegetables.

Turkey Heart Goulash

Yield:
Serves 6

Prep Time:
20 minutes

Cook Time:
1 hour 10 minutes

Total Time:
1 hour 30 minutes

Nutritional Information
(per serving,
approximately):

🔥 **Calories: 240**

Fat: 15g
Carbohydrates: 8g net
(10g total carbs minus 2g
fiber)
Protein: 20g

Ingredients:

1 pound turkey hearts, cleaned and cut into bite-sized pieces

2 tablespoons olive oil

1 large onion, chopped

3 cloves garlic, minced

2 tablespoons paprika (preferably Hungarian)

1 teaspoon caraway seeds

1/2 teaspoon dried thyme

1 red bell pepper, chopped

1 green bell pepper, chopped

2 medium zucchinis, diced

1 cup sliced mushrooms

1 can (14 oz) diced tomatoes, no sugar added

3 cups beef broth (or chicken broth)

Salt and pepper to taste

Sour cream (for garnish)

Fresh parsley, chopped (for garnish)

1. **Heat oil and sauté onions:**
   - In a large pot or Dutch oven, heat the olive oil over medium heat. Add the onion and garlic, sautéing until the onion is translucent, about 5 minutes.

2. **Brown the turkey hearts:**
   - Increase the heat to medium-high and add the turkey hearts to the pot. Cook until they are browned on all sides, about 10 minutes.

3. **Add spices and vegetables:**
   - Stir in the paprika, caraway seeds, and thyme, cooking for about 1 minute until fragrant.
   - Add the red and green bell peppers, zucchinis, and mushrooms. Cook for another 5-7 minutes until the vegetables begin to soften.

4. **Simmer the goulash:**
   - Add the diced tomatoes and beef broth. Bring to a boil, then reduce the heat to low. Cover and simmer for about 45 minutes, or until the turkey hearts are tender and the flavors have melded.

5. **Final seasoning and serving:**
   - Season with salt and pepper to taste.
   - Serve hot, garnished with a dollop of sour cream and a sprinkle of fresh parsley.

Turkey Liver Stroganoff

Yield:
Serves 4

Prep Time:
15 minutes

Cook Time:
20 minutes

Total Time:
35 minutes

Nutritional Information
(per serving,
approximately):

🔥 **Calories: 300**

Fat: 20g
Carbohydrates: 5g net
Protein: 25g

Ingredients:

1 pound turkey liver, cleaned and cut into bite-sized pieces

3 tablespoons butter

1 large onion, thinly sliced

2 cloves garlic, minced

1 cup mushrooms, sliced

1 teaspoon paprika

1/2 cup beef broth (or chicken broth)

1/2 cup sour cream

Salt and pepper to taste

2 tablespoons fresh parsley, chopped (for garnish)

1 tablespoon olive oil (if needed)

1. **Prepare the liver:**
   - Rinse the turkey liver under cold water and pat dry. Ensure it's cleaned properly, removing any connective tissue.

2. **Cook the onions and mushrooms:**
   - In a large skillet, melt 2 tablespoons of butter over medium heat. Add the onion and garlic, sautéing until the onion is soft and translucent, about 5 minutes.
   - Add the mushrooms and continue to cook until the mushrooms are browned and their moisture has evaporated, about 5-7 minutes.

3. **Sauté the liver:**
   - Push the onion and mushrooms to the side of the skillet. Add the remaining tablespoon of butter and the liver pieces. Increase the heat to medium-high and sear the liver until browned on all sides, about 3-4 minutes. Do not overcook to keep the liver tender.

4. **Add liquids and seasonings:**
   - Sprinkle the paprika over the liver and vegetables. Stir in the beef broth and bring to a simmer. Reduce the heat to low and let simmer for 3-5 minutes, just until the liver is cooked through.

5. **Finish with sour cream:**
   - Remove the skillet from heat. Stir in the sour cream and season with salt and pepper to taste. Mix gently until everything is well combined and creamy.

6. **Serve:**
   - Garnish with chopped parsley. Serve hot over a bed of keto-friendly noodles, zucchini noodles, or simply enjoy it as is.

CHAPTER 4

Beef, Lamb & Pork

Lamb Chops with Rosemary and Garlic

Yield:
Serves 4

Prep Time:
10 minutes

Cook Time:
15 minutes

Total Time:
25 minutes

Nutritional Information
(per serving):

🔥 **Calories: 400**

Total Fat: 30g
Saturated Fat: 13g
Cholesterol: 105mg
Sodium: 85mg
Total Carbohydrates: 1g
Dietary Fiber: 0.2g
Sugars: 0g
Protein: 30g

Ingredients:

8 lamb chops (approximately 2 lbs)

4 tablespoons olive oil

4 cloves garlic, minced

2 tablespoons fresh rosemary, finely chopped

Salt and freshly ground black pepper, to taste

1 teaspoon red pepper flakes (optional for a spicy kick)

1. **Preparation:**
   - In a small bowl, combine olive oil, minced garlic, chopped rosemary, salt, black pepper, and red pepper flakes (if using). Mix well to create the marinade.

2. **Marinate the Lamb:**
   - Place the lamb chops in a large bowl or a resealable plastic bag. Pour the marinade over the chops, ensuring they are well coated. Seal the bag or cover the bowl and refrigerate for at least 1 hour, or up to overnight for deeper flavor.

3. **Cook the Lamb:**
   - Preheat a grill or skillet over medium-high heat. Remove the lamb chops from the marinade, letting the excess oil drip off (discard the remaining marinade). Place the lamb chops on the hot grill or skillet.

4. **Grilling/Searing:**
   - Cook the lamb chops for about 3 to 4 minutes on each side for medium-rare, or adjust the cooking time according to your preferred doneness.

5. **Rest the Meat:**
   - Once cooked to your liking, transfer the lamb chops to a plate and let them rest for about 5 minutes. This helps the juices redistribute, ensuring a moist and flavorful chop.

6. **Serve:**
   - Serve the lamb chops hot, garnished with additional rosemary sprigs if desired.

Meatballs

Yield:
Makes about 20 meatballs

Prep Time:
15 minutes

Cook Time:
25 minutes

Total Time:
40 minutes

Nutritional Information
(per serving –
2 meatballs):

🔥 **Calories: 210**

Total Fat: 15g
Saturated Fat: 5g
Cholesterol: 72mg
Sodium: 290mg
Total Carbohydrates: 2g
Dietary Fiber: 1g
Sugars: 0g
Protein: 16g

Ingredients:

1 pound ground beef (preferably lean)

1/2 cup almond flour

1/4 cup grated Parmesan cheese

1 large egg

2 cloves garlic, minced

1 teaspoon dried oregano

1 teaspoon dried basil

1/2 teaspoon onion powder

1/2 teaspoon salt

1/4 teaspoon black pepper

1 tablespoon olive oil

1 (24 oz) jar low-carb marinara sauce (optional, for serving)

Fresh parsley, chopped (for garnish)

1. **Preheat oven:**
   - Preheat your oven to 400°F (200°C). Line a baking sheet with parchment paper or lightly grease it with olive oil.

2. **Preparation:**
   - In a large mixing bowl, combine the ground beef, almond flour, Parmesan cheese, egg, minced garlic, dried oregano, dried basil, onion powder, salt, and black pepper. Mix everything together until well combined.
   - Shape the mixture into meatballs, about 1 to 1.5 inches in diameter, and place them on the prepared baking sheet.
   - Brush the meatballs lightly with olive oil to help them brown in the oven.

3. **Bake in the oven:**
   - Bake the meatballs in the preheated oven for 20-25 minutes, or until they are cooked through and nicely browned on the outside.

4. **Rest the meatballs:**
   - Once the meatballs are cooked, remove them from the oven and let them rest for a few minutes.

5. **Serve:**
   - Serve the meatballs hot, garnished with fresh chopped parsley. You can enjoy them on their own as a snack or appetizer, or serve them with low-carb marinara sauce for dipping or over zucchini noodles for a complete meal.

Pork Schnitzel

Yield:
Serves 4

Prep Time:
15 minutes

Cook Time:
15 minutes

Total Time:
30 minutes

Nutritional Information
(per serving):

🔥 Calories: 395

Total Fat: 27g
Saturated Fat: 6g
Cholesterol: 178mg
Sodium: 500mg
Total Carbohydrates: 4g
Dietary Fiber: 1g
Sugars: 0g
Protein: 34g

Ingredients:

4 boneless pork chops (about 4 oz each), pounded to 1/4-inch thickness

1/2 cup almond flour

1/4 cup grated Parmesan cheese

1 teaspoon paprika

1/2 teaspoon garlic powder

1/2 teaspoon onion powder

1/2 teaspoon dried thyme

1/2 teaspoon salt

1/4 teaspoon black pepper

2 large eggs, beaten

1/4 cup olive oil, for frying

Lemon wedges, for serving

Fresh parsley, chopped (for garnish)

1. **Preparation:**
   - In a shallow dish, combine the almond flour, Parmesan cheese, paprika, garlic powder, onion powder, dried thyme, salt, and black pepper. Mix well to combine.
   - Place the beaten eggs in another shallow dish.

2. **Preheat the pan:**
   - Heat the olive oil in a large skillet over medium-high heat.
   - Dredge each pork chop in the beaten eggs, then coat it in the almond flour mixture, pressing gently to adhere the coating to the meat.
   - Once the oil is hot, carefully place the coated pork chops in the skillet. You may need to work in batches to avoid overcrowding the pan.
   - Cook the pork chops for 3-4 minutes on each side, or until they are golden brown and cooked through. The internal temperature should reach 145°F (63°C).
   - Once cooked, transfer the pork schnitzels to a plate lined with paper towels to drain any excess oil.

3. **Serve:**
   - Serve the pork schnitzels hot, garnished with fresh chopped parsley and lemon wedges on the side.

Italian Stuffed Bell Peppers

Yield:
Serves 4

Prep Time:
20 minutes

Cook Time:
40 minutes

Total Time:
1 hour

Nutritional Information
(per serving –
1 stuffed pepper):

🔥 Calories: 380

Total Fat: 26g
Saturated Fat: 10g
Cholesterol: 75mg
Sodium: 780mg
Total Carbohydrates: 11g
Dietary Fiber: 3g
Sugars: 5g
Protein: 24g

Ingredients:

4 large bell peppers, any color

1 tablespoon olive oil

1 small onion, finely chopped

2 cloves garlic, minced

1 pound ground Italian sausage (or ground beef)

1/2 cup marinara sauce (look for low-carb or sugar-free options)

1 cup cauliflower rice

1/2 cup shredded mozzarella cheese

1/4 cup grated Parmesan cheese

1 teaspoon dried oregano

1 teaspoon dried basil

Salt and black pepper, to taste

Fresh parsley, chopped (for garnish)

1. **Preheat oven:** Preheat your oven to 375°F (190°C). Grease a baking dish large enough to hold the bell peppers.

2. **Preparation:**
   - Cut the tops off the bell peppers and remove the seeds and membranes. Set aside.
   - Heat olive oil in a large skillet over medium heat. Add the chopped onion and minced garlic, and sauté until softened, about 2-3 minutes.
   - Add the ground Italian sausage (or beef) to the skillet, breaking it up with a spoon, and cook until browned and cooked through, about 5-7 minutes.
   - Stir in the marinara sauce and cauliflower rice. Season with dried oregano, dried basil, salt, and black pepper. Cook for another 5 minutes, allowing the flavors to meld together.
   - Remove the skillet from the heat and stir in the shredded mozzarella cheese until melted.

3. **Stuff:**
   - Stuff each bell pepper with the sausage mixture, pressing down gently to pack it in. Place the stuffed peppers upright in the prepared baking dish.
   - Sprinkle the grated Parmesan cheese over the tops of the stuffed peppers.

4. **Bake in the oven:**
   - Cover the baking dish with foil and bake in the preheated oven for 25-30 minutes, or until the peppers are tender.
   - Remove the foil and bake for an additional 5-10 minutes, or until the cheese is golden and bubbly.
   - Once cooked, remove the stuffed peppers from the oven and let them cool for a few minutes.

5. **Serve:** Serve the stuffed peppers hot, garnished with fresh chopped parsley.

Bacon-Wrapped Pork Tenderloin

Yield:
Serves 4

Prep Time:
15 minutes

Cook Time:
30 minutes

Total Time:
45 minutes

Nutritional Information
(per serving):

🔥 Calories: 370

Total Fat: 23g
Saturated Fat: 7g
Cholesterol: 100mg
Sodium: 480mg
Total Carbohydrates: 1g
Dietary Fiber: 0g
Sugars: 0g
Protein: 38g

Ingredients:

1 pork tenderloin (about 1 pound)

8 slices bacon

2 tablespoons olive oil

2 cloves garlic, minced

1 teaspoon dried thyme

1 teaspoon dried rosemary

Salt and black pepper, to taste

Fresh parsley, chopped (for garnish)

1. **Preheat oven:**
   - Preheat your oven to 400°F (200°C). Line a baking sheet with aluminum foil or parchment paper.

2. **Marinate:**
   - In a small bowl, mix together the minced garlic, dried thyme, dried rosemary, salt, and black pepper.
   - Pat the pork tenderloin dry with paper towels. Rub the olive oil all over the pork tenderloin, then season it with the garlic and herb mixture, making sure to coat it evenly.
   - Wrap the bacon slices around the pork tenderloin, securing them with toothpicks if needed. Place the bacon-wrapped pork tenderloin on the prepared baking sheet.

3. **Bake in the oven:**
   - Roast the pork tenderloin in the preheated oven for 25-30 minutes, or until the internal temperature reaches 145°F (63°C) for medium rare or 160°F (71°C) for medium, and the bacon is crispy.
   - Once cooked, remove the pork tenderloin from the oven and let it rest for a few minutes before slicing.

4. **Serve:**
   - Slice the bacon-wrapped pork tenderloin into thick slices and arrange them on a serving platter.
   - Garnish with chopped fresh parsley before serving.

Almond and Caraway Crusted Steak

Yield:
Serves 2

Prep Time:
10 minutes

Cook Time:
15 minutes

Total Time:
25 minutes

Nutritional Information
(per serving):

🔥 Calories: 480

Total Fat: 35g
Saturated Fat: 8g
Cholesterol: 110mg
Sodium: 630mg
Total Carbohydrates: 5g
Dietary Fiber: 3g
Sugars: 0g
Protein: 36g

Ingredients:

2 steaks of your choice (such as ribeye, sirloin, or filet mignon), about 8 oz each

1/4 cup almond flour

2 tablespoons ground almonds

1 tablespoon caraway seeds, crushed

1 teaspoon garlic powder

1/2 teaspoon onion powder

1/2 teaspoon salt

1/4 teaspoon black pepper

2 tablespoons olive oil

1. **Preheat oven:**
   - Preheat your oven to 400°F (200°C). Line a baking sheet with parchment paper or aluminum foil.

2. **Marinate:**
   - In a shallow dish, combine the almond flour, ground almonds, crushed caraway seeds, garlic powder, onion powder, salt, and black pepper. Mix well to combine.
   - Pat the steaks dry with paper towels.
   - Brush each steak with olive oil, then press both sides of the steaks into the almond and caraway mixture, coating them evenly.

3. **Heat a skillet:**
   - Heat a skillet over medium-high heat. Once hot, add the steaks to the skillet and sear them for 2-3 minutes on each side, or until they develop a golden-brown crust.
   - Transfer the seared steaks to the prepared baking sheet and place them in the preheated oven.

4. **Bake the steaks:**
   - Bake the steaks in the oven for 8-10 minutes for medium-rare, or adjust the cooking time according to your desired level of doneness.
   - Once cooked to your liking, remove the steaks from the oven and let them rest for a few minutes before serving.

5. **Serve:**
   - Serve the almond and caraway crusted steaks hot, with your favorite keto-friendly side dishes.

Almond Butter Beef Stew

Yield:
Serves 6

Prep Time:
15 minutes

Cook Time:
2 hours

Total Time:
2 hours 15 minutes

Nutritional Information
(per serving):

🔥 Calories: 420

Total Fat: 29g
Saturated Fat: 8g
Cholesterol: 90mg
Sodium: 690mg
Total Carbohydrates: 8g
Dietary Fiber: 3g
Sugars: 3g
Protein: 34g

Ingredients:

2 pounds beef stew meat, cubed
2 tablespoons olive oil
1 onion, diced
3 cloves garlic, minced
2 medium carrots, sliced
2 celery stalks, sliced
1 tablespoon tomato paste

4 cups beef broth
1 teaspoon dried thyme
1 teaspoon dried rosemary
1/2 teaspoon paprika
Salt and black pepper, to taste
1/2 cup almond butter
Fresh parsley, chopped (for garnish)

1. **1. Preparation:**
   - In a large pot or Dutch oven, heat the olive oil over medium-high heat. Add the cubed beef stew meat and brown on all sides, about 5-7 minutes. Remove the meat from the pot and set aside.

2. **Simmer:**
   - In the same pot, add the diced onion and minced garlic. Sauté until softened and fragrant, about 2-3 minutes.
   - Add the sliced carrots and celery to the pot, and cook for another 5 minutes, stirring occasionally.
   - Stir in the tomato paste and cook for 1-2 minutes to allow it to caramelize slightly.
   - Return the browned beef stew meat to the pot. Pour in the beef broth and add the dried thyme, dried rosemary, paprika, salt, and black pepper. Stir to combine.
   - Bring the stew to a simmer, then reduce the heat to low. Cover and let it simmer gently for 1.5 to 2 hours, or until the meat is tender.
   - Once the meat is tender, stir in the almond butter until well incorporated. Adjust seasoning with salt and pepper if needed.
   - Continue to simmer the stew for another 10-15 minutes to allow the flavors to meld together.

3. **Serve:**
   - Serve the almond butter beef stew hot, garnished with fresh chopped parsley.

Beef Burgers with Lettuce & Avocado

Yield:
Makes 4 burgers

Prep Time:
10 minutes

Cook Time:
10 minutes

Total Time:
20 minutes

Nutritional Information
(per serving - 1 burger):

🔥 Calories: 320

Total Fat: 24g
Saturated Fat: 9g
Cholesterol: 80mg
Sodium: 80mg
Total Carbohydrates: 4g
Dietary Fiber: 3g
Sugars: 0g
Protein: 23g

Ingredients:

1 pound ground beef (preferably 80/20)

1 teaspoon garlic powder

1 teaspoon onion powder

1/2 teaspoon paprika

Salt and black pepper, to taste

4 large lettuce leaves (such as butter or romaine)

1 ripe avocado, sliced

Optional toppings: sliced cheese, bacon, tomato slices, onion slices

---

1. **Preparation:**
   - In a mixing bowl, combine the ground beef with garlic powder, onion powder, paprika, salt, and black pepper. Mix well until the seasonings are evenly distributed throughout the meat.
   - Divide the seasoned ground beef into 4 equal portions. Shape each portion into a patty, about 1/2 to 3/4 inch thick.

2. **Heat a grill, grill pan:**
   - Heat a grill, grill pan, or skillet over medium-high heat. If using a grill, lightly oil the grates to prevent sticking.
   - Place the beef patties on the preheated grill or skillet. Cook the burgers for 4-5 minutes on each side, or until they reach your desired level of doneness. For medium-rare, aim for an internal temperature of 130-135°F (55-57°C); for medium, aim for 140-145°F (60-63°C); and for well-done, aim for 160°F (71°C).

3. **Serve:**
   - While the burgers are cooking, prepare the lettuce leaves and avocado slices.
   - Once the burgers are cooked to your liking, remove them from the heat and let them rest for a few minutes.
   - To assemble the burgers, place each beef patty on a lettuce leaf. Top with sliced avocado and any other desired toppings.
   - Serve the keto beef burgers with lettuce and avocado immediately.

Garlic Pork Chops with Mint Pesto

Yield:
4 servings

Prep Time:
15 minutes

Cook Time:
15 minutes

Total Time:
30 minutes

Nutritional Information
(per serving):

🔥 **Calories: 520**

Protein: 29 g
Fat: 43 g
Carbohydrates: 3 g
Fiber: 1 g
Net Carbs: 2 g

Ingredients:

For the Pork Chops:

4 boneless pork chops, about 1-inch thick

2 tablespoons olive oil

4 cloves garlic, minced

Salt and black pepper, to taste

For the Mint Pesto:

1 cup fresh mint leaves

1/2 cup fresh basil leaves

1/4 cup parmesan cheese, grated

1/4 cup almonds, chopped

2 cloves garlic

1/2 cup olive oil

Juice of 1 lemon

Salt and pepper, to taste

1. **Preheat the Grill:**
   - Preheat your grill or skillet over medium-high heat.

2. **Prepare Pork Chops:**
   - Rub each pork chop with olive oil and minced garlic. Season generously with salt and pepper. Let them marinate while you make the pesto.

3. **Make Mint Pesto:**
   - In a food processor, combine mint leaves, basil leaves, parmesan cheese, almonds, and garlic. Pulse until coarsely chopped. With the processor running, slowly pour in the olive oil and lemon juice until the mixture is well blended but still has some texture. Season with salt and pepper to taste.

4. **Cook Pork Chops:**
   - Place pork chops on the hot grill or skillet. Cook for about 7-8 minutes on each side, or until the internal temperature reaches 145°F (63°C). Remove from heat and let rest for a few minutes.

5. **Serve:**
   - Spoon the mint pesto over the cooked pork chops and serve immediately.

Ground Beef Stew with Marjoram and Basil

Yield:
4 servings

Prep Time:
10 minutes

Cook Time:
30 minutes

Total Time:
40 minutes

Nutritional Information
(per serving):

🔥 **Calories: 300**

Protein: 22 g
Fat: 20 g
Carbohydrates: 8 g
Fiber: 2 g
Net Carbs: 6 g

Ingredients:

1 pound ground beef (preferably lean)

2 tablespoons olive oil

1 medium onion, chopped

2 cloves garlic, minced

1 red bell pepper, chopped

2 cups beef broth (low sodium)

1 can (14.5 ounces) diced tomatoes, no added sugar

1 teaspoon dried marjoram

1 teaspoon dried basil

Salt and pepper, to taste

1/2 cup chopped fresh basil (for garnish)

1. **Brown the Ground Beef:**
   - In a large pot, heat 1 tablespoon of olive oil over medium heat. Add the ground beef and cook until browned, breaking it up with a spoon as it cooks. Once browned, remove the beef from the pot and set aside.

2. **Sauté Vegetables:**
   - In the same pot, add the remaining tablespoon of olive oil. Add the chopped onion and garlic, and sauté until the onions become translucent, about 5 minutes. Add the chopped red bell pepper and cook for another 3 minutes.

3. **Combine Ingredients:**
   - Return the browned ground beef to the pot. Add the beef broth and diced tomatoes. Stir in the dried marjoram and basil. Season with salt and pepper to taste. Bring to a simmer.

4. **Simmer the Stew:**
   - Reduce heat and let the stew simmer for about 20 minutes, or until the vegetables are tender and the flavors have melded together.

5. **Garnish and Serve:**
   - Just before serving, stir in the fresh chopped basil for added freshness. Adjust seasoning if necessary.

Cider-Herb Pork Tenderloin

Yield:
4 servings

Prep Time:
10 minutes

Cook Time:
25 minutes

Total Time:
35 minutes

Nutritional Information
(per serving):

🔥 Calories: 310

Protein: 25 g
Fat: 21 g
Carbohydrates: 5 g
Fiber: 0 g
Net Carbs: 5 g

Ingredients:

1 pork tenderloin (about 1 to 1.5 pounds)

Salt and pepper, to taste

2 tablespoons olive oil

1 cup unsweetened apple cider (look for a low-carb version)

1 tablespoon fresh rosemary, finely chopped

1 tablespoon fresh thyme, finely chopped

2 cloves garlic, minced

1 tablespoon Dijon mustard

1/2 cup heavy cream

1. **Preheat Oven:**
   - Preheat your oven to 375°F (190°C).

2. **Prepare the Pork:**
   - Season the pork tenderloin generously with salt and pepper.

3. **Sear the Pork:**
   - In a large ovenproof skillet, heat the olive oil over medium-high heat. Add the pork tenderloin and sear on all sides until golden brown, about 2-3 minutes per side.

4. **Make the Sauce:**
   - Remove the pork from the skillet and set aside. In the same skillet, add the apple cider, rosemary, thyme, and garlic. Bring to a simmer and let it reduce slightly, about 5 minutes. Stir in the Dijon mustard and heavy cream, and bring back to a simmer.

5. **Roast the Pork:**
   - Return the pork to the skillet. Spoon some of the sauce over the pork. Transfer the skillet to the oven and roast for 15-18 minutes, or until the pork reaches an internal temperature of 145°F (63°C).

6. **Rest and Serve:**
   - Let the pork rest for a few minutes before slicing. Serve with the cider-herb sauce drizzled over the top.

Coconut-Olive Beef with Mushrooms

Yield:
4 servings

Prep Time:
15 minutes

Cook Time:
20 minutes

Total Time:
35 minutes

Nutritional Information
(per serving):

🔥 **Calories: 360**

Protein: 24 g
Fat: 27 g
Carbohydrates: 6 g
Fiber: 1 g
Net Carbs: 5 g

Ingredients:

1 pound beef strips (suitable for stir-fry)

2 tablespoons coconut oil

1 medium onion, sliced

3 cloves garlic, minced

1 cup sliced mushrooms

1/2 cup green olives, pitted and sliced

1 can (14 ounces) full-fat coconut milk

1 teaspoon dried thyme

Salt and pepper, to taste

Fresh parsley, chopped (for garnish)

1. **Prep Ingredients:**
   - Start by preparing all your ingredients. Slice the beef into thin strips, slice the onion, mince the garlic, and slice the mushrooms and olives.

2. **Brown the Beef:**
   - In a large skillet or frying pan, heat the coconut oil over medium-high heat. Add the beef strips and sear them until they are browned on all sides, about 3-4 minutes. Remove the beef from the pan and set aside.

3. **Sauté Vegetables:**
   - In the same pan, add the onion and garlic, cooking until the onion becomes translucent, about 5 minutes. Add the mushrooms and continue to cook until the mushrooms are soft, about 5 more minutes.

4. **Combine Ingredients:**
   - Return the beef to the pan. Add the sliced olives, coconut milk, and thyme. Season with salt and pepper to taste. Stir well to combine.

5. **Simmer:**
   - Reduce the heat to low and let the mixture simmer gently for about 10 minutes, or until the sauce has thickened slightly and the beef is tender.

6. **Garnish and Serve:**
   - Garnish with chopped fresh parsley before serving. Serve hot.

Beef Ragout with Pepper and Green Beans

Yield:
4 servings

Prep Time:
10 minutes

Cook Time:
30 minutes

Total Time:
40 minutes

Nutritional Information
(per serving):

🔥 **Calories: 300**

Protein: 28 g
Fat: 18 g
Carbohydrates: 10 g
Fiber: 3 g
Net Carbs: 7 g

Ingredients:

1 pound beef stew meat, cut into small chunks

2 tablespoons olive oil

1 large onion, diced

2 cloves garlic, minced

1 red bell pepper, cut into strips

2 cups green beans, trimmed and halved

1 can (14.5 ounces) diced tomatoes, no sugar added

1 cup beef broth

1 teaspoon dried thyme

1 teaspoon dried rosemary

Salt and pepper, to taste

1. **Brown the Beef:**
   - In a large pot or Dutch oven, heat the olive oil over medium-high heat. Add the beef chunks and brown them on all sides, about 5-7 minutes. Remove the beef from the pot and set aside.

2. **Sauté Vegetables:**
   - In the same pot, add the onion and garlic. Cook until the onion is translucent, about 5 minutes. Add the red bell pepper and green beans, cooking for another 5 minutes until they start to soften.

3. **Add Beef and Simmer:**
   - Return the beef to the pot along with the diced tomatoes and beef broth. Stir in the thyme and rosemary. Season with salt and pepper to taste. Bring to a boil, then reduce heat to low and let it simmer, covered, for about 20 minutes or until the beef is tender and the flavors have melded.

4. **Final Adjustments:**
   - Check the seasoning and adjust with more salt and pepper if needed. The ragout should be thick and hearty, with vegetables that are tender but still vibrant.

Sausage & Zucchini Lasagna

Yield:
6 servings

Prep Time:
20 minutes

Cook Time:
45 minutes

Total Time:
1 hour 5 minutes

Nutritional Information
(per serving):

🔥 **Calories: 390**

Protein: 24 g
Fat: 28 g
Carbohydrates: 8 g
Fiber: 2 g
Net Carbs: 6 g

Ingredients:

4 medium zucchinis, sliced lengthwise into thin strips

1 pound Italian sausage, casing removed

1 cup ricotta cheese

1 cup shredded mozzarella cheese

1/2 cup grated Parmesan cheese

1 egg

2 cups marinara sauce (sugar-free)

1 tablespoon olive oil

2 cloves garlic, minced

1 teaspoon dried oregano

1 teaspoon dried basil

Salt and pepper, to taste

1. **Preheat Oven and Prepare Zucchini:**
   - Preheat your oven to 375°F (190°C). Lightly salt the zucchini slices and set them aside for 10 minutes to draw out moisture. Pat them dry with paper towels to remove excess water.

2. **Cook Sausage:**
   - In a skillet over medium heat, add the olive oil and sausage. Break it apart with a spoon and cook until browned and cooked through. Add the minced garlic, oregano, and basil, and cook for another 2 minutes. Set aside.

3. **Prepare Cheese Mixture:** In a bowl, mix together the ricotta cheese, Parmesan cheese, egg, salt, and pepper until well combined.

4. **Assemble Lasagna:**
   - In a 9x13 inch baking dish, spread a thin layer of marinara sauce. Layer zucchini strips over the sauce to cover the bottom of the dish. Spread half of the sausage mixture over the zucchini, then dollop half of the ricotta mixture on top and gently spread. Sprinkle a third of the mozzarella cheese over this. Repeat the layers once more, ending with a final layer of zucchini strips. Top with the remaining marinara sauce and sprinkle with the remaining mozzarella cheese.

5. **Bake:** Cover the dish with foil and bake in the preheated oven for 30 minutes. Remove the foil and bake for an additional 15 minutes, or until the cheese is bubbly and golden brown.

6. **Cool and Serve:** Let the lasagna cool for 10 minutes before slicing and serving. This helps the layers set and makes it easier to serve.

Creamy Pork Chops

Yield:
4 servings

Prep Time:
10 minutes

Cook Time:
20 minutes

Total Time:
30 minutes

Nutritional Information
(per serving):

🔥 **Calories: 520**

Protein: 31 g
Fat: 44 g
Carbohydrates: 3 g
Fiber: 0 g
Net Carbs: 3 g

Ingredients:

4 boneless pork chops, about 1-inch thick

Salt and pepper, to taste

1 tablespoon olive oil

2 tablespoons butter

3 cloves garlic, minced

1 cup heavy cream

1/2 cup chicken broth

1 teaspoon Dijon mustard

1 teaspoon dried thyme

1/2 teaspoon paprika

1/4 cup grated Parmesan cheese

1. **Prepare Pork Chops:**
   - Season the pork chops generously with salt and pepper on both sides.

2. **Cook Pork Chops:**
   - In a large skillet, heat the olive oil over medium-high heat. Add the pork chops and sear until golden brown on each side, about 3-4 minutes per side. Remove the pork chops from the skillet and set aside.

3. **Make the Sauce:**
   - In the same skillet, reduce the heat to medium and add the butter. Once melted, add the minced garlic and sauté until fragrant, about 1 minute. Pour in the heavy cream and chicken broth, and stir in the Dijon mustard, thyme, and paprika. Bring to a simmer.

4. **Simmer the Sauce:**
   - Let the sauce simmer for about 5 minutes, or until it begins to thicken. Stir in the grated Parmesan cheese until it's fully incorporated and the sauce is creamy.

5. **Finish Cooking:**
   - Return the pork chops to the skillet, coating them in the sauce. Cook for another 3-5 minutes, or until the pork chops are fully cooked (internal temperature should reach 145°F).

6. **Serve:**
   - Serve the pork chops with a generous amount of the creamy sauce spooned over the top.

Lamb Curry

Yield:
4 servings

Prep Time:
15 minutes

Cook Time:
1 hour

Total Time:
1 hour 15 minutes

Nutritional Information
(per serving):

♦ Calories: 560

Protein: 38 g
Fat: 42 g
Carbohydrates: 13 g
Fiber: 3 g
Net Carbs: 10 g

Ingredients:
1.5 pounds lamb shoulder, cut into 1-inch cubes
2 tablespoons coconut oil
1 large onion, finely chopped
3 cloves garlic, minced
1-inch piece of ginger, grated
1 tablespoon curry powder
1 teaspoon turmeric powder
1 teaspoon cumin powder
1 teaspoon coriander powder
1/2 teaspoon cayenne pepper (adjust to taste)
1 can (14 oz) diced tomatoes, no added sugar
1 can (14 oz) coconut milk
Salt and pepper, to taste
Fresh cilantro, chopped (for garnish)

1. **Brown the Lamb:**
   - In a large pot or Dutch oven, heat the coconut oil over medium-high heat. Add the lamb cubes and season with salt and pepper. Brown the lamb on all sides, about 5-7 minutes. Remove the lamb from the pot and set aside.

2. **Sauté Aromatics:**
   - In the same pot, reduce the heat to medium. Add the chopped onion, garlic, and ginger, and sauté until the onions are translucent, about 5 minutes.

3. **Add Spices:**
   - Stir in the curry powder, turmeric, cumin, coriander, and cayenne pepper. Cook for another minute until the spices are fragrant.

4. **Simmer the Curry:**
   - Return the browned lamb to the pot. Add the diced tomatoes and coconut milk. Stir to combine all the ingredients. Bring the mixture to a boil, then reduce the heat to low and cover. Let the curry simmer gently for about 45 minutes or until the lamb is tender.

5. **Finish and Serve:**
   - Check the seasoning and adjust salt and pepper as needed. Garnish with chopped fresh cilantro before serving.

Lamb Meatballs with Feta Cheese

Yield:
4 servings

Prep Time:
15 minutes

Cook Time:
25 minutes

Total Time:
40 minutes

Nutritional Information
(per serving):

🔥 Calories: 410

Protein: 24 g
Fat: 34 g
Carbohydrates: 3 g
Fiber: 1 g
Net Carbs: 2 g

Ingredients:

1 pound ground lamb
1/2 cup feta cheese, crumbled
1/4 cup almond flour
1 large egg
2 cloves garlic, minced
1 tablespoon fresh mint, finely chopped
1 tablespoon fresh oregano, finely chopped
1 teaspoon salt
1/2 teaspoon black pepper
2 tablespoons olive oil

1. **Preheat Oven:**
   - Preheat your oven to 375°F (190°C).

2. **Mix Ingredients:**
   - In a large bowl, combine the ground lamb, feta cheese, almond flour, egg, minced garlic, mint, oregano, salt, and pepper. Mix everything together until well combined.

3. **Form Meatballs:**
   - Shape the mixture into balls, about the size of a golf ball.

4. **Cook Meatballs:**
   - Heat the olive oil in a large oven-proof skillet over medium-high heat. Add the meatballs and brown them on all sides, about 5-7 minutes.

5. **Bake:**
   - Transfer the skillet to the preheated oven and bake the meatballs for 15-18 minutes, or until they are cooked through and reach an internal temperature of 160°F (71°C).

6. **Serve:**
   - Serve the lamb meatballs hot, garnished with additional chopped mint or oregano if desired.

Spiced Ground Lamb with Cauliflower Rice

Yield:
4 servings

Prep Time:
10 minutes

Cook Time:
20 minutes

Total Time:
30 minutes

Nutritional Information
(per serving):

🔥 **Calories: 380**

Protein: 23 g
Fat: 27 g
Carbohydrates: 12 g
Fiber: 4 g
Net Carbs: 8 g

Ingredients:

For the Spiced Ground Lamb:
1 pound ground lamb
1 tablespoon olive oil
1 large onion, finely chopped
3 cloves garlic, minced
1 teaspoon ground cumin
1 teaspoon smoked paprika
1/2 teaspoon ground cinnamon
1/2 teaspoon ground coriander

Salt and pepper, to taste
1/4 cup fresh cilantro, chopped
1/4 cup fresh mint, chopped

For the Cauliflower Rice:
1 large head cauliflower, grated or processed into rice-sized pieces
1 tablespoon olive oil
Salt and pepper, to taste

1. **Cook the Lamb:**
   - In a large skillet, heat the olive oil over medium heat. Add the onion and garlic, sautéing until the onion becomes translucent, about 5 minutes. Add the ground lamb, breaking it up with a spoon. Cook until browned, about 7-8 minutes.

2. **Add Spices:**
   - Stir in cumin, paprika, cinnamon, and coriander. Season with salt and pepper. Cook for another 2-3 minutes until the spices are well incorporated and fragrant. Remove from heat and stir in the chopped cilantro and mint.

3. **Prepare Cauliflower Rice:**
   - Heat another tablespoon of olive oil in a separate skillet over medium heat. Add the grated cauliflower and season with salt and pepper. Cook, stirring occasionally, until the cauliflower is tender and has a slightly golden color, about 5-8 minutes.

4. **Serve:**
   - Spoon the spiced ground lamb over the cauliflower rice. Garnish with additional herbs if desired.

Beef and Broccoli Stir-Fry

Yield:
4 servings

Prep Time:
15 minutes

Cook Time:
15 minutes

Total Time:
30 minutes

Nutritional Information
(per serving):

🔥 **Calories: 330**

Protein: 26 g
Fat: 21 g
Carbohydrates: 8 g
Fiber: 2 g
Net Carbs: 6 g

Ingredients:

1 pound beef sirloin or flank steak, thinly sliced against the grain

3 cups broccoli florets

2 tablespoons olive oil

1 tablespoon ginger, minced

3 cloves garlic, minced

For the Sauce:

1/3 cup soy sauce (or coconut aminos for a soy-free option)

1/4 cup beef broth

2 tablespoons sesame oil

1 tablespoon apple cider vinegar

1 tablespoon erythritol or another keto-friendly sweetener

1 teaspoon xanthan gum (optional, for thickening)

1. **Prepare the Sauce:**

   • In a small bowl, whisk together the soy sauce, beef broth, sesame oil, apple cider vinegar, erythritol, and xanthan gum (if using). Set aside.

2. **Cook the Beef:**

   • Heat one tablespoon of olive oil in a large skillet or wok over medium-high heat. Add the beef slices and cook until browned and cooked through, about 3-4 minutes per side. Remove the beef from the skillet and set aside.

3. **Sauté Vegetables:**

   • In the same skillet, add the remaining tablespoon of olive oil. Add the minced ginger and garlic, sautéing until fragrant, about 1 minute. Add the broccoli florets and stir-fry until they are bright green and slightly tender, about 5 minutes.

4. **Combine and Simmer:**

   • Return the beef to the skillet with the broccoli. Pour the sauce over the top and stir to combine. Reduce the heat to medium-low and let the mixture simmer for 3-5 minutes, or until the sauce has thickened to your liking and the broccoli is tender but still crisp.

5. **Serve:**

   • Serve the beef and broccoli stir-fry hot, optionally garnishing with sesame seeds or sliced green onions.

Beef Stuffed Zucchini Boats

Yield:
4 servings

Prep Time:
15 minutes

Cook Time:
25 minutes

Total Time:
40 minutes

Nutritional Information
(per serving):

🔥 **Calories: 380**

Protein: 26 g
Fat: 25 g
Carbohydrates: 12 g
Fiber: 3 g
Net Carbs: 9 g

Ingredients:

4 medium zucchini

1 pound ground beef

1 tablespoon olive oil

1 small onion, diced

2 cloves garlic, minced

1 bell pepper, diced

1 cup canned diced tomatoes, drained

1 teaspoon dried oregano

1 teaspoon dried basil

Salt and pepper, to taste

1/2 cup shredded mozzarella cheese

2 tablespoons grated Parmesan cheese

Fresh parsley, chopped (for garnish)

1. **Preheat Oven and Prepare Zucchini:**
   - Preheat your oven to 375°F (190°C). Cut the zucchini in half lengthwise and scoop out the flesh with a spoon to create a 'boat', leaving about 1/4 inch of zucchini flesh on the skin. Chop the scooped-out flesh and set aside for use in the filling.

2. **Cook the Beef:**
   - In a large skillet, heat the olive oil over medium heat. Add the onion and garlic, sautéing until the onion becomes translucent, about 5 minutes. Add the ground beef and cook until browned, breaking it up as it cooks. Drain any excess fat.

3. **Add Vegetables and Seasonings:**
   - To the skillet with the beef, add the chopped zucchini flesh, bell pepper, diced tomatoes, oregano, basil, salt, and pepper. Cook for about 5 minutes until the vegetables are just tender.

4. **Stuff the Zucchini:**
   - Spoon the beef and vegetable mixture into the hollowed-out zucchini boats. Place the stuffed zucchini in a baking dish.

5. **Add Cheese and Bake:**
   - Sprinkle the shredded mozzarella and Parmesan cheese over the top of each stuffed zucchini. Bake in the preheated oven for about 20 minutes, or until the zucchini is tender and the cheese is bubbly and golden.

6. **Garnish and Serve:**
   - Garnish with fresh chopped parsley before serving.

CHAPTER 5

Fish & Seafood

Crispy Salmon with Broccoli & Bell Pepper

Yield:
Serves 4

Prep Time:
15 minutes

Cook Time:
20 minutes

Total Time:
35 minutes

Nutritional Information
(per serving):

🔥 **Calories: 350**

Protein: 34 g
Fat: 22 g
Carbohydrates: 9 g
(net carbs)
Fiber: 4 g
Sugar: 3 g

Ingredients:

4 salmon fillets (about 6 ounces each)

1 large head of broccoli, cut into florets

1 red bell pepper, thinly sliced

1 yellow bell pepper, thinly sliced

2 tablespoons olive oil

Salt and pepper, to taste

1 teaspoon garlic powder

1 teaspoon onion powder

1 lemon, sliced (for garnish)

Fresh dill or parsley, for garnish (optional)

1. **Preheat the Oven:**
   - Preheat your oven to 400°F (200°C).

2. **Prepare the Vegetables:**
   - On a large baking sheet, toss the broccoli and bell peppers with 1 tablespoon of olive oil, salt, and pepper.

3. **Season the Salmon:**
   - Rub the salmon fillets with the remaining tablespoon of olive oil. Season each fillet with garlic powder, onion powder, salt, and pepper. Arrange the seasoned salmon fillets on the baking sheet with the vegetables.

4. **Bake:**
   - Place the baking sheet in the oven and bake for about 18-20 minutes, or until the salmon is cooked through and flakes easily with a fork, and the vegetables are tender and slightly charred.

5. **Garnish and Serve:**
   - Remove from the oven and garnish with lemon slices and fresh herbs, if using. Serve immediately.

Dilled Salmon in Creamy Sauce

Yield:
Serves 4

Prep Time:
10 minutes

Cook Time:
15 minutes

Total Time:
25 minutes

Nutritional Information
(per serving):

🔥 Calories: 380

Protein: 34 g
Fat: 26 g
Carbohydrates: 2 g
(net carbs)
Fiber: 0 g
Sugar: 1 g

Ingredients:

4 salmon fillets (about 6 ounces each)

1 tablespoon olive oil

Salt and pepper, to taste

1/2 cup heavy cream

1/4 cup chicken broth

2 tablespoons fresh dill, chopped

1 tablespoon lemon juice

1 teaspoon garlic, minced

1/2 teaspoon onion powder

Lemon slices and additional dill for garnish

1. **Cook the Salmon:**
   - Heat the olive oil in a large skillet over medium-high heat.
   - Season the salmon fillets with salt and pepper.
   - Place the salmon, skin side up, in the skillet. Cook for 3-4 minutes on each side or until golden and cooked through. Remove from the skillet and set aside.

2. **Make the Creamy Dill Sauce:**
   - In the same skillet, reduce the heat to medium. Add the garlic and sauté for about 1 minute until fragrant.
   - Stir in the heavy cream, chicken broth, lemon juice, dill, and onion powder. Bring to a simmer.
   - Cook for 3-5 minutes, stirring occasionally, until the sauce thickens slightly.

3. **Combine and Serve:**
   - Return the salmon to the skillet, spooning the sauce over the fillets.
   - Simmer for an additional 2-3 minutes to allow the salmon to soak up some of the flavors.
   - Garnish with lemon slices and additional chopped dill before serving.

Baked Cod with Parmesan and Almonds

Yield:
Serves 4

Prep Time:
10 minutes

Cook Time:
15 minutes

Total Time:
25 minutes

Nutritional Information
(per serving):

🔥 **Calories: 280**

Protein: 28 g
Fat: 16 g
Carbohydrates: 3 g
(net carbs)
Fiber: 1 g
Sugar: 0 g

Ingredients:

4 cod fillets (about 6 ounces each)
Salt and pepper, to taste
1/2 cup grated Parmesan cheese
1/4 cup almond flour
1/4 cup sliced almonds

2 tablespoons unsalted butter, melted
1 teaspoon garlic powder
1 tablespoon fresh parsley, chopped
Lemon wedges, for serving

1. **Preheat the Oven and Prepare Baking Sheet:**
   - Preheat your oven to 400°F (200°C). Lightly grease a baking sheet or line with parchment paper.

2. **Prepare the Topping:**
   - In a small bowl, mix together the grated Parmesan, almond flour, sliced almonds, melted butter, and garlic powder.

3. **Season the Cod:**
   - Season the cod fillets with salt and pepper on both sides and place them on the prepared baking sheet.

4. **Apply the Topping:**
   - Evenly distribute the Parmesan and almond mixture over the top of each cod fillet, pressing slightly to adhere.

5. **Bake:**
   - Place in the oven and bake for about 12-15 minutes, or until the fish flakes easily with a fork and the topping is golden and crispy.

6. **Garnish and Serve:**
   - Garnish with chopped parsley and serve with lemon wedges on the side.

Pan-Seared Lemon-Garlic Salmon

Yield:
Serves 4

Prep Time:
5 minutes

Cook Time:
10 minutes

Total Time:
15 minutes

Nutritional Information
(per serving):

🔥 Calories: 295

Protein: 34 g
Fat: 17 g
Carbohydrates: 2 g
(net carbs)
Fiber: 0.5 g
Sugar: 1 g

Ingredients:

4 salmon fillets (about 6 ounces each)

Salt and pepper, to taste

2 tablespoons olive oil

4 cloves garlic, minced

1 lemon, juiced and zested

1/4 cup chicken broth

1 tablespoon fresh parsley, chopped

Lemon slices, for garnish

1. **Season the Salmon:**
   - Season the salmon fillets with salt and pepper on both sides.

2. **Heat the Oil:**
   - Heat the olive oil in a large skillet over medium-high heat.

3. **Cook the Salmon:**
   - Add the salmon fillets to the skillet, skin-side up, and cook for 4-5 minutes on each side or until golden and cooked through.

4. **Make the Sauce:**
   - Remove the salmon and set aside. In the same skillet, add the minced garlic and sauté for 1 minute until fragrant.
   - Pour in the lemon juice and chicken broth, and bring to a simmer. Scrape up any browned bits from the bottom of the skillet.
   - Stir in the lemon zest and cook for another 2 minutes until the sauce is slightly reduced.

5. **Serve:**
   - Return the salmon to the skillet, spoon the sauce over the fillets.
   - Garnish with fresh parsley and lemon slices.

Keto Fish Tacos

Yield:
Serves 4

Prep Time:
15 minutes

Cook Time:
10 minutes

Total Time:
25 minutes

Nutritional Information
(per serving, 2 tacos each):

🔥 **Calories: 350**

Protein: 28 g
Fat: 22 g
Carbohydrates: 12 g
(net carbs)
Fiber: 8 g
Sugar: 2 g

Ingredients:

4 large white fish fillets (such as cod or tilapia)

1 tablespoon olive oil

1 teaspoon chili powder

1 teaspoon cumin

1/2 teaspoon garlic powder

Salt and pepper, to taste

8 keto tortillas (made from almond flour or coconut flour)

1/2 small cabbage, shredded

1 avocado, sliced

1/4 cup cilantro, chopped

1 lime, cut into wedges

Lime Crema:

1/2 cup sour cream

1 tablespoon lime juice

Zest of 1 lime

Salt, to taste

1. **Prepare the Fish:**
   - In a small bowl, mix chili powder, cumin, garlic powder, salt, and pepper.
   - Rub the spice mix all over the fish fillets.

2. **Cook the Fish:**
   - Heat olive oil in a large skillet over medium-high heat.
   - Place the fish in the skillet and cook for about 4-5 minutes on each side, until cooked through and easily flaked with a fork. Remove from the heat and break the fish into chunks.

3. **Make Lime Crema:**
   - In a small bowl, combine sour cream, lime juice, lime zest, and salt. Stir until smooth.

4. **Assemble the Tacos:**
   - Warm the keto tortillas according to the package instructions.
   - Divide the cooked fish among the tortillas.
   - Top with shredded cabbage, sliced avocado, and chopped cilantro.
   - Drizzle lime crema over the top.

5. **Serve:**
   - Serve with lime wedges on the side.

Keto Seafood Chowder

Yield:
Serves 6

Prep Time:
15 minutes

Cook Time:
25 minutes

Total Time:
40 minutes

Nutritional Information
(per serving):

🔥 Calories: 310

Protein: 20 g
Fat: 24 g
Carbohydrates: 7 g
(net carbs)
Fiber: 2 g
Sugar: 3 g

Ingredients:

2 tablespoons butter
1 medium onion, diced
2 celery stalks, chopped
2 cloves garlic, minced
1/2 teaspoon paprika
1/2 teaspoon dried thyme
1 bay leaf
3 cups fish or seafood stock

1 cup heavy cream
1 pound mixed seafood (shrimp, scallops, and any firm white fish), cut into bite-sized pieces
1/2 head cauliflower, cut into small florets
Salt and pepper, to taste
Fresh parsley, chopped (for garnish)

1. **Sauté Vegetables:**
   - In a large pot, melt butter over medium heat. Add the onion and celery, and cook until softened, about 5 minutes. Add the garlic, paprika, and thyme, and cook for an additional minute until fragrant.

2. **Add Liquids and Simmer:**
   - Stir in the fish or seafood stock, heavy cream, and bay leaf. Bring the mixture to a simmer.

3. **Cook the Cauliflower:**
   - Add the cauliflower florets to the pot. Simmer for about 10 minutes or until the cauliflower is tender.

4. **Add the Seafood:**
   - Add the mixed seafood to the pot. Cook for about 5 minutes or until the seafood is cooked through and opaque.

5. **Season and Serve:**
   - Remove the bay leaf, and season the chowder with salt and pepper to taste. Serve hot, garnished with chopped parsley.

Spicy Tuna Stuffed Avocados

Yield:
Serves 4

Prep Time:
10 minutes

Cook Time:
0 minutes

Total Time:
10 minutes

Nutritional Information
(per serving):

🔥 **Calories: 300**

Protein: 10 g
Fat: 26 g
Carbohydrates: 8 g
(net carbs)
Fiber: 6 g
Sugar: 1 g

Ingredients:

2 large avocados, halved and pitted

1 can (5 ounces) tuna in water, drained

1/4 cup mayonnaise

1 tablespoon sriracha sauce (adjust based on spice preference)

1 tablespoon lime juice

2 tablespoons red onion, finely chopped

2 tablespoons cilantro, chopped

Salt and pepper, to taste

1 teaspoon sesame seeds (optional, for garnish)

1. **Prepare the Avocados:**
   - Scoop out some of the avocado flesh to create more space for the filling, leaving a small border around the edges. Chop the scooped-out flesh and set aside.

2. **Mix the Tuna Filling:**
   - In a bowl, mix the drained tuna, mayonnaise, sriracha, lime juice, red onion, cilantro, and the chopped avocado. Stir until well combined. Season with salt and pepper to taste.

3. **Stuff the Avocados:**
   - Spoon the tuna mixture into the hollowed-out avocado halves. Ensure the mixture is packed well and mounded slightly on top.

4. **Garnish and Serve:**
   - Sprinkle sesame seeds over the stuffed avocados for an extra touch of texture and flavor.
   - Serve immediately or chill in the refrigerator for a refreshing and cool snack.

Sushi Rolls

Yield:
Serves 2

Prep Time:
20 minutes

Cook Time:
0 minutes

Total Time:
20 minutes

Nutritional Information
(per serving):

🔥 **Calories: 300**

Protein: 25 g
Fat: 20 g
Carbohydrates: 5 g
(net carbs)
Fiber: 3 g
Sugar: 2 g

Ingredients:

1 large cucumber

1/2 pound sushi-grade tuna or salmon, thinly sliced

1/2 avocado, thinly sliced

2 ounces cream cheese, cut into strips

1 tablespoon soy sauce or tamari (for dipping)

1 teaspoon wasabi paste (optional, for serving)

1 tablespoon pickled ginger (optional, for serving)

Sesame seeds (optional, for garnish)

1. **Prepare the Cucumber:**
   - Use a vegetable peeler to peel the cucumber into long, thin, wide strips. Lay the strips on paper towels to absorb any excess moisture.

2. **Assemble the Rolls:**
   - Take a cucumber strip and lay it flat on a clean surface.
   - At one end of the cucumber strip, place a few slices of tuna or salmon, a couple of avocado slices, and a strip of cream cheese.
   - Carefully roll the cucumber around the filling, starting from the end with the filling and rolling towards the empty end to create a tight roll.

3. **Serve:**
   - Cut each roll into bite-sized pieces, similar to traditional sushi rolls.
   - Serve with soy sauce or tamari for dipping, and optionally with wasabi and pickled ginger on the side.
   - Sprinkle sesame seeds over the rolls for garnish if desired.

Grilled Octopus with Olive Oil and Lemon

Yield:
Serves 4

Prep Time:
10 minutes
(plus time for marinating if preferred)

Cook Time:
20 minutes

Total Time:
30 minutes

Nutritional Information
(per serving):

◊ Calories: 250
Protein: 25 g
Fat: 15 g
Carbohydrates: 5 g
(net carbs)
Fiber: 0 g
Sugar: 1 g

Ingredients:

2 pounds octopus, cleaned and pre-cooked

1/4 cup extra virgin olive oil, plus extra for drizzling

2 lemons, one juiced and one cut into wedges

4 cloves garlic, minced

1 teaspoon dried oregano

Salt and pepper, to taste

Fresh parsley, chopped (for garnish)

1. **Prepare the Octopus:**
   - If the octopus is not pre-cooked, boil it in a large pot of salted water with a cork (to tenderize) for about 40-60 minutes until tender, then let it cool and cut into pieces.
   - Marinate (Optional):
   - In a bowl, combine olive oil, lemon juice, minced garlic, oregano, salt, and pepper. Add the octopus pieces and marinate for at least 30 minutes, or overnight in the refrigerator for enhanced flavor.

2. **Preheat the Grill:**
   - Heat your grill to medium-high heat.

3. **Grill the Octopus:**
   - Remove the octopus from the marinade and grill for about 4-5 minutes on each side or until the octopus starts to char and crisp on the edges.

4. **Serve:**
   - Drizzle the grilled octopus with a bit more olive oil and squeeze fresh lemon over the top. Garnish with chopped parsley and serve with lemon wedges on the side.

Parmesan Shrimp Scampi Pizza

Yield:
Serves 4

Prep Time:
15 minutes

Cook Time:
20 minutes

Total Time:
35 minutes

Nutritional Information
(per serving):

🔥 **Calories: 400**

Protein: 28 g
Fat: 30 g
Carbohydrates: 5 g
(net carbs)
Fiber: 2 g
Sugar: 1 g

Ingredients:

For the Keto Pizza Crust:
1 1/2 cups mozzarella cheese, shredded
2 tablespoons cream cheese
3/4 cup almond flour
1 egg
1/2 teaspoon garlic powder

For the Topping:
1 tablespoon olive oil

2 cloves garlic, minced
1/2 pound shrimp, peeled and deveined
1/4 cup Parmesan cheese, grated
1/4 cup mozzarella cheese, shredded
1 tablespoon fresh parsley, chopped
Red pepper flakes, to taste
Salt and pepper, to taste
Lemon wedges, for serving

1. **Prepare the Keto Crust:**
   - Preheat your oven to 425°F (220°C).
   - In a microwave-safe bowl, combine mozzarella and cream cheese. Microwave for about 1 minute, stir, and microwave again for another 30 seconds.
   - Stir in almond flour, egg, and garlic powder. Mix until well combined.
   - Place the dough between two pieces of parchment paper and roll into a pizza shape. Remove the top parchment and transfer the dough (on the bottom parchment) to a baking sheet.
   - Bake for 10 minutes, until slightly golden.

2. **Cook the Shrimp:**
   - While the crust is baking, heat olive oil in a skillet over medium heat.
   - Add garlic and sauté until fragrant, about 1 minute.
   - Add the shrimp, season with salt, pepper, and red pepper flakes. Cook until the shrimp are pink and opaque, about 2-3 minutes per side. Remove from heat.

3. **Assemble the Pizza:**
   - Sprinkle half of the Parmesan cheese over the pre-baked crust.
   - Spread the cooked shrimp evenly over the crust, then top with mozzarella and the remaining Parmesan.
   - Return to the oven and bake for another 10 minutes or until the cheese is bubbly and golden.

4. **Finish and Serve:**
   - Garnish with chopped parsley.
   - Serve hot with lemon wedges on the side for squeezing over the top.

Spicy Keto Fish Stew

Yield:
Serves 4

Prep Time:
15 minutes

Cook Time:
25 minutes

Total Time:
40 minutes

Nutritional Information
(per serving):

🔥 **Calories: 240**

Protein: 28 g
Fat: 9 g
Carbohydrates: 10 g
(net carbs)
Fiber: 2 g
Sugar: 5 g

Ingredients:

1 tablespoon olive oil

1 medium onion, diced

2 cloves garlic, minced

1 bell pepper, diced (any color)

1 teaspoon smoked paprika

1/2 teaspoon cayenne pepper (adjust based on spice preference)

1 teaspoon ground cumin

1 can (14.5 ounces) diced tomatoes, no sugar added

2 cups fish or seafood broth

1 pound firm white fish (like cod or halibut), cut into chunks

1/2 pound shrimp, peeled and deveined

Salt and pepper, to taste

2 tablespoons fresh cilantro, chopped

1 lime, cut into wedges for serving

1. **Sauté Vegetables:**
   - Heat the olive oil in a large pot over medium heat. Add the onion and bell pepper, and sauté until softened, about 5 minutes.
   - Add the garlic, smoked paprika, cayenne pepper, and cumin. Cook for another 2 minutes until fragrant.

2. **Add Liquids and Simmer:**
   - Stir in the diced tomatoes and fish broth. Bring to a simmer.

3. **Add the Seafood:**
   - Add the fish chunks and shrimp to the pot. Season with salt and pepper. Simmer gently for about 15 minutes, or until the fish is cooked through and the shrimp are opaque.

4. **Finish and Serve:**
   - Stir in the chopped cilantro. Taste and adjust seasoning if necessary.
   - Serve the stew hot, with lime wedges on the side for squeezing over each serving.

Lemon Garlic Mussels

Yield:
Serves 4

Prep Time:
10 minutes

Cook Time:
10 minutes

Total Time:
20 minutes

Nutritional Information
(per serving):

◊ Calories: 240

Protein: 20 g
Fat: 12 g
Carbohydrates: 6 g
(net carbs)
Fiber: 0 g
Sugar: 1 g

Ingredients:

2 pounds fresh mussels, cleaned and debearded

2 tablespoons butter

1 tablespoon olive oil

4 cloves garlic, minced

1 small shallot, minced

1/2 cup dry white wine (suitable for keto, like a dry Sauvignon Blanc)

1 lemon, juiced and zested

1/4 cup fresh parsley, chopped

Salt and pepper, to taste

Lemon wedges, for serving

1. **Prepare the Mussels:**
   - Rinse and scrub the mussels under cold water. Pull off any beards and discard any mussels that do not close when tapped.

2. **Cook Garlic and Shallots:**
   - In a large pot, heat the butter and olive oil over medium heat. Add the garlic and shallot, and sauté until soft and fragrant, about 2-3 minutes.

3. **Steam the Mussels:**
   - Increase the heat to high and add the white wine, lemon juice, and lemon zest. Bring to a boil.
   - Add the mussels, cover the pot, and let them steam until they open, about 5-7 minutes. Discard any mussels that do not open.

4. **Finish and Serve:**
   - Stir in the chopped parsley and season with salt and pepper.
   - Serve the mussels hot, with the broth and lemon wedges on the side for squeezing over the mussels.

Crab Cakes

Yield:
Serves 4

Prep Time:
15 minutes

Cook Time:
10 minutes

Total Time:
25 minutes

Nutritional Information
(per serving):

🔥 **Calories: 290**

Protein: 20 g
Fat: 22 g
Carbohydrates: 3 g
(net carbs)
Fiber: 1 g
Sugar: 1 g

Ingredients:

1 pound lump crab meat, carefully picked through for shells

1/4 cup almond flour

1/4 cup mayonnaise

1 egg, beaten

2 tablespoons green onions, finely chopped

1 teaspoon Dijon mustard

1 teaspoon Worcestershire sauce

1/2 teaspoon paprika

1/4 teaspoon garlic powder

Salt and pepper, to taste

2 tablespoons olive oil, for frying

Lemon wedges and fresh parsley, for serving

1. **Mix Ingredients:**
   - In a large bowl, combine the crab meat, almond flour, mayonnaise, beaten egg, green onions, Dijon mustard, Worcestershire sauce, paprika, garlic powder, salt, and pepper. Mix gently until well combined, taking care not to break up the crab meat too much.

2. **Form the Crab Cakes:**
   - Shape the mixture into 8 small patties, about 1/2 inch thick.

3. **Cook the Crab Cakes:**
   - Heat the olive oil in a large skillet over medium heat.
   - Once hot, add the crab cakes and cook for about 4–5 minutes on each side, or until they are golden brown and cooked through.

4. **Serve:**
   - Serve the crab cakes hot, garnished with lemon wedges and fresh parsley.

Keto Tuna Salad

 Yield:
Serves 4

 Prep time:
10 minutes

 Cook time:
0 minutes

 Total Time:
10 minutes

Nutritional Information
(per serving):

🔥 **Calories: 230**

Protein: 20 g | Fat: 15 g |
Carbohydrates: 3 g
(net carbs) | Fiber: 1 g |
Sugar: 1 g

Ingredients:

2 cans of tuna in olive oil (5 ounces each), drained

1/4 cup mayonnaise (preferably avocado oil mayonnaise)

1 celery stalk, finely chopped

2 tablespoons red onion, finely chopped

1 tablespoon fresh parsley, chopped

1 tablespoon Dijon mustard

1 tablespoon lemon juice

Salt and pepper, to taste

1 avocado, diced (optional for serving)

Lettuce leaves (optional for serving)

1. **Combine Ingredients:** In a medium bowl, mix together the drained tuna, mayonnaise, chopped celery, red onion, parsley, Dijon mustard, and lemon juice. Stir until all ingredients are well combined.

2. **Season:** Season the salad with salt and pepper to taste.

3. **Optional Additions:** If desired, gently fold in diced avocado for extra creaminess and healthy fats.

4. **Serve:** Serve the tuna salad on its own, or scoop onto lettuce leaves for a low-carb wrap.

Pan-Seared Tuna Steak

 Yield:
Serves 2

 Prep time:
5 minutes

 Cook time:
6 minutes

 Total Time:
11 minutes

Nutritional Information
(per serving):

🔥 **Calories: 290**

Protein: 40 g | Fat: 14 g |
Carbohydrates: 1 g
(net carbs) | Fiber: 0 g |
Sugar: 0 g

Ingredients:

2 tuna steaks (about 6 ounces each)

1 tablespoon olive oil

Salt and freshly ground black pepper, to taste

1 teaspoon garlic powder

1 tablespoon sesame seeds (optional, for garnish)

1 tablespoon fresh parsley, chopped (for garnish)

Lemon wedges, for serving

1. **Prepare the Tuna Steaks:** Pat the tuna steaks dry with paper towels. Season both sides with salt, pepper, and garlic powder.

2. **Heat the Pan:** Heat the olive oil in a skillet over high heat until it is just starting to smoke.

3. **Cook the Tuna:** Place the tuna steaks in the hot skillet. Sear them for about 3 minutes on each side for medium-rare, or adjust the cooking time to your preferred level of doneness.

4. **Garnish and Serve:**
   - Sprinkle the tuna steaks with sesame seeds and chopped parsley for garnish.
   - Serve immediately with lemon wedges on the side.

CHAPTER 6

Spicy (exotic) recipes

Not for every day

Grilled Octopus with Olive Oil and Lemon

Yield:
4 servings

Prep Time:
20 minutes
(plus 1 hour
marinating time)

Cook Time:
30 minutes

Total Time:
1 hour 50 minutes

Nutritional Information
(per serving):

🔥 **Calories: 210**

Total Fat: 14g
Saturated Fat: 2g
Cholesterol: 96mg
Sodium: 320mg
Total Carbohydrates: 2g
Dietary Fiber: 0g
Sugars: 0g
Protein: 18g

Ingredients:

2 pounds octopus, cleaned
1/4 cup olive oil
3 cloves garlic, minced
1 lemon, juiced

1 tablespoon lemon zest
1 teaspoon dried oregano
Salt and pepper to taste
Fresh parsley, chopped (for garnish)

1. **Prep the Octopus:**
   - If the octopus isn't already cleaned, remove the beak, eyes, and innards. Rinse thoroughly under cold water.

2. **Marinate the Octopus:**
   - In a large bowl, combine the olive oil, minced garlic, lemon juice, lemon zest, dried oregano, salt, and pepper.
   - Add the octopus to the bowl and toss to coat. Cover and marinate in the refrigerator for at least 1 hour, preferably overnight for more flavor.

3. **Pre-cook the Octopus:**
   - Fill a large pot with water and bring it to a boil. Add the octopus and cook for about 20-30 minutes, or until tender. The time will vary depending on the size of the octopus.
   - Drain and let the octopus cool slightly. Cut into manageable pieces if necessary.

4. **Grill the Octopus:**
   - Preheat your grill to medium-high heat.
   - Once the grill is hot, place the octopus on the grill and cook for 3-4 minutes per side, or until charred and crispy.

5. **Serve:**
   - Remove the octopus from the grill and place it on a serving platter.
   - Drizzle with a bit more olive oil, sprinkle with chopped fresh parsley, and serve with extra lemon wedges on the side.

Octopus Salad with Avocado and Cucumbers

Yield:
4 servings

Prep Time:
20 minutes
(plus 1 hour
marinating time)

Cook Time:
30 minutes

Total Time:
1 hour 50 minutes

Nutritional Information
(per serving):

🔥 **Calories: 250**

Total Fat: 18g
Saturated Fat: 2.5g
Cholesterol: 96mg
Sodium: 320mg
Total Carbohydrates: 8g
Dietary Fiber: 4g
Sugars: 2g
Protein: 18g

Ingredients:

2 pounds octopus, cleaned
1 avocado, diced
1 cucumber, diced
1/4 red onion, thinly sliced
1/4 cup olive oil
2 tablespoons lemon juice

1 tablespoon red wine vinegar
1 teaspoon Dijon mustard
1 clove garlic, minced
1 teaspoon dried oregano
Salt and pepper to taste
Fresh parsley, chopped (for garnish)

1. **Prep the Octopus:**
   - If the octopus isn't already cleaned, remove the beak, eyes, and innards. Rinse thoroughly under cold water.

2. **Marinate the Octopus:**
   - In a large bowl, combine the olive oil, minced garlic, lemon juice, dried oregano, salt, and pepper.
   - Add the octopus to the bowl and toss to coat. Cover and marinate in the refrigerator for at least 1 hour, preferably overnight for more flavor.

3. **Pre-cook the Octopus:**
   - Fill a large pot with water and bring it to a boil. Add the octopus and cook for about 20-30 minutes, or until tender. The time will vary depending on the size of the octopus.
   - Drain and let the octopus cool slightly. Cut into bite-sized pieces.

4. **Prepare the Salad:**
   - In a large salad bowl, combine the diced avocado, diced cucumber, and thinly sliced red onion.
   - In a small bowl, whisk together the olive oil, lemon juice, red wine vinegar, Dijon mustard, and a pinch of salt and pepper to make the dressing.

5. **Assemble the Salad:**
   - Add the octopus pieces to the salad bowl with the vegetables.
   - Pour the dressing over the salad and toss gently to combine.

6. **Serve:**
   - Garnish with fresh chopped parsley and serve immediately.

Octopus and Cauliflower Stew

Yield:
4 servings

Prep Time:
20 minutes

Cook Time:
1 hour

Total Time:
1 hour 20 minutes

Nutritional Information
(per serving):

🔥 **Calories: 220**

Total Fat: 12g
Saturated Fat: 2g
Cholesterol: 96mg
Sodium: 480mg
Total Carbohydrates: 10g
Dietary Fiber: 4g
Sugars: 4g
Protein: 20g

Ingredients:

2 pounds octopus, cleaned

1 head of cauliflower, cut into florets

1 onion, chopped

2 cloves garlic, minced

1 can (14.5 oz) diced tomatoes

4 cups chicken or vegetable broth

1/4 cup olive oil

1 tablespoon tomato paste

1 teaspoon smoked paprika

1 teaspoon dried oregano

1 bay leaf

Salt and pepper to taste

Fresh parsley, chopped (for garnish)

Lemon wedges (for serving)

1. **Prep the Octopus:**
    - If the octopus isn't already cleaned, remove the beak, eyes, and innards. Rinse thoroughly under cold water.

2. **Pre-cook the Octopus:**
    - Fill a large pot with water and bring it to a boil. Add the octopus and cook for about 20-30 minutes, or until tender. The time will vary depending on the size of the octopus.
    - Drain and let the octopus cool slightly. Cut into bite-sized pieces.

3. **Prepare the Stew Base:**
    - In a large pot or Dutch oven, heat the olive oil over medium heat. Add the chopped onion and minced garlic and sauté until the onion is translucent, about 5 minutes.
    - Stir in the tomato paste and cook for another 2 minutes.

4. **Cook the Stew:**
    - Add the diced tomatoes, smoked paprika, dried oregano, bay leaf, and chicken or vegetable broth to the pot. Stir to combine.
    - Add the pre-cooked octopus pieces and cauliflower florets to the pot. Bring to a boil, then reduce the heat to low and let simmer for about 30 minutes, or until the cauliflower is tender and the flavors have melded together.
    - Season with salt and pepper to taste.

5. **Serve:**
    - Ladle the stew into bowls and garnish with fresh chopped parsley.
    - Serve with lemon wedges on the side for an extra burst of flavor.

Smoked Paprika Octopus

Yield:
4 servings

Prep Time:
20 minutes
(plus 1 hour
marinating time)

Cook Time:
40 minutes

Total Time:
2 hours

Nutritional Information
(per serving):

🔥 **Calories: 220**

Total Fat: 14g
Saturated Fat: 2g
Cholesterol: 96mg
Sodium: 320mg
Total Carbohydrates: 3g
Dietary Fiber: 1g
Sugars: 1g
Protein: 18g

Ingredients:

2 pounds octopus, cleaned
1/4 cup olive oil
2 tablespoons smoked paprika
1 tablespoon lemon juice
1 tablespoon lemon zest

2 cloves garlic, minced
1 teaspoon dried oregano
Salt and pepper to taste
Fresh parsley, chopped (for garnish)
Lemon wedges (for serving)

1. **Prep the Octopus:**
   - If the octopus isn't already cleaned, remove the beak, eyes, and innards. Rinse thoroughly under cold water.

2. **Marinate the Octopus:**
   - In a large bowl, combine the olive oil, smoked paprika, lemon juice, lemon zest, minced garlic, dried oregano, salt, and pepper.
   - Add the octopus to the bowl and toss to coat. Cover and marinate in the refrigerator for at least 1 hour, preferably overnight for more flavor.

3. **Pre-cook the Octopus:**
   - Fill a large pot with water and bring it to a boil. Add the octopus and cook for about 20-30 minutes, or until tender. The time will vary depending on the size of the octopus.
   - Drain and let the octopus cool slightly. Cut into manageable pieces if necessary.

4. **Grill the Octopus:**
   - Preheat your grill to medium-high heat.
   - Once the grill is hot, place the octopus on the grill and cook for 3-4 minutes per side, or until charred and crispy.

5. **Serve:**
   - Remove the octopus from the grill and place it on a serving platter.
   - Garnish with fresh chopped parsley and serve with lemon wedges on the side for an extra burst of flavor.

Crab Avocado Salad

Yield:
4 servings

Prep Time:
15 minutes

Cook Time:
None

Total Time:
15 minutes

Nutritional Information
(per serving):

🔥 **Calories: 250**

Total Fat: 18g
Saturated Fat: 3g
Cholesterol: 85mg
Sodium: 520mg
Total Carbohydrates: 8g
Dietary Fiber: 5g
Sugars: 1g
Protein: 17g

Ingredients:

1 pound lump crab meat, picked over for shells

2 ripe avocados, diced

1 cucumber, diced

1/4 red onion, finely chopped

1/4 cup fresh cilantro, chopped

1/4 cup mayonnaise

2 tablespoons lime juice

1 teaspoon lime zest

1 tablespoon olive oil

Salt and pepper to taste

Lime wedges (for serving)

1. **Prepare the Dressing:**
   - In a small bowl, whisk together the mayonnaise, lime juice, lime zest, olive oil, salt, and pepper until well combined.

2. **Assemble the Salad:**
   - In a large bowl, gently combine the lump crab meat, diced avocados, diced cucumber, finely chopped red onion, and chopped fresh cilantro.

3. **Mix the Salad:**
   - Pour the dressing over the crab and avocado mixture. Gently toss to combine, ensuring all ingredients are evenly coated with the dressing.

4. **Serve:**
   - Divide the salad into four servings. Garnish with additional cilantro if desired and serve with lime wedges on the side for an extra burst of flavor.

Lemon Garlic Crab Legs

Yield:
4 servings

Prep Time:
10 minutes

Cook Time:
15 minutes

Total Time:
25 minutes

Nutritional Information
(per serving):

🔥 **Calories: 250**

Total Fat: 15g
Saturated Fat: 8g
Cholesterol: 110mg
Sodium: 720mg
Total Carbohydrates: 1g
Dietary Fiber: 0g
Sugars: 0g
Protein: 24g

Ingredients:

2 pounds crab legs (King or Snow)
1/4 cup butter, melted
3 cloves garlic, minced
2 tablespoons lemon juice
1 tablespoon lemon zest

1 teaspoon dried parsley
Salt and pepper to taste
Lemon wedges (for serving)
Fresh parsley, chopped (for garnish)

1. **Preheat the Oven:**
   - Preheat your oven to 375°F (190°C).

2. **Prepare the Crab Legs:**
   - If the crab legs are frozen, thaw them in the refrigerator or under cold running water.

3. **Make the Lemon Garlic Butter:**
   - In a small bowl, combine the melted butter, minced garlic, lemon juice, lemon zest, dried parsley, salt, and pepper. Mix well.

4. **Season the Crab Legs:**
   - Place the crab legs on a baking sheet or in a large baking dish. Brush the lemon garlic butter mixture generously over the crab legs, ensuring they are well coated.

5. **Bake the Crab Legs:**
   - Cover the baking sheet or dish with aluminum foil and bake in the preheated oven for 12–15 minutes, or until the crab legs are heated through.

6. **Serve:**
   - Remove the crab legs from the oven and transfer them to a serving platter.
   - Garnish with fresh chopped parsley and serve with lemon wedges on the side.

Creamy Mussels with Bacon

Yield:
4 servings

Prep Time:
15 minutes

Cook Time:
20 minutes

Total Time:
35 minutes

Nutritional Information
(per serving):

🔥 Calories: 390

Total Fat: 30g
Saturated Fat: 15g
Cholesterol: 130mg
Sodium: 820mg
Total Carbohydrates: 6g
Dietary Fiber: 0g
Sugars: 2g
Protein: 24g

Ingredients:

2 pounds mussels, cleaned and debearded
4 slices bacon, chopped
1 small onion, finely chopped
2 cloves garlic, minced
1 cup heavy cream
1/2 cup chicken broth
1/4 cup dry white wine
2 tablespoons butter
1 tablespoon lemon juice
1 teaspoon lemon zest
Salt and pepper to taste
Fresh parsley, chopped (for garnish)

1. **Cook the Bacon:**
   - In a large pot or Dutch oven, cook the chopped bacon over medium heat until crispy. Remove the bacon with a slotted spoon and set aside, leaving the bacon fat in the pot.

2. **Sauté the Aromatics:**
   - Add the finely chopped onion to the pot with the bacon fat and sauté until translucent, about 5 minutes. Add the minced garlic and cook for another 1-2 minutes until fragrant.

3. **Deglaze the Pot:**
   - Pour in the dry white wine and chicken broth, scraping up any browned bits from the bottom of the pot. Bring to a simmer.

4. **Add the Mussels:**
   - Add the cleaned and debearded mussels to the pot. Cover and cook for about 5-7 minutes, or until the mussels have opened. Discard any mussels that do not open.

5. **Make the Creamy Sauce:**
   - Remove the mussels with a slotted spoon and set aside. Stir in the heavy cream, butter, lemon juice, and lemon zest. Simmer for 3-5 minutes until the sauce thickens slightly. Season with salt and pepper to taste.

6. **Combine and Serve:**
   - Return the mussels to the pot and gently toss to coat them in the creamy sauce. Stir in the cooked bacon.
   - Transfer the mussels to serving bowls, garnish with fresh chopped parsley, and serve immediately.

Curried Mussels

Yield:
4 servings

Prep Time:
15 minutes

Cook Time:
20 minutes

Total Time:
35 minutes

Nutritional Information
(per serving):

🔥 **Calories: 350**

Total Fat: 25g
Saturated Fat: 20g
Cholesterol: 90mg
Sodium: 620mg
Total Carbohydrates: 9g
Dietary Fiber: 2g
Sugars: 2g
Protein: 23g

Ingredients:

2 pounds mussels, cleaned and debearded

2 tablespoons coconut oil

1 small onion, finely chopped

3 cloves garlic, minced

1 tablespoon ginger, minced

1 tablespoon curry powder

1 teaspoon turmeric

1 teaspoon ground cumin

1 can (14 oz) coconut milk

1/2 cup chicken or vegetable broth

1 tablespoon lime juice

Salt and pepper to taste

Fresh cilantro, chopped (for garnish)

Lime wedges (for serving)

1. **Prep the Mussels:**
   - If the mussels are not cleaned, scrub them under cold water and remove any beards.

2. **Sauté the Aromatics:**
   - In a large pot or Dutch oven, heat the coconut oil over medium heat. Add the finely chopped onion and sauté until translucent, about 5 minutes. Add the minced garlic and ginger, and cook for another 1-2 minutes until fragrant.

3. **Add the Spices:**
   - Stir in the curry powder, turmeric, and ground cumin. Cook for 1-2 minutes to toast the spices and enhance their flavors.

4. **Create the Curry Base:**
   - Pour in the coconut milk and chicken or vegetable broth, stirring well to combine. Bring to a simmer.

5. **Cook the Mussels:**
   - Add the cleaned mussels to the pot. Cover and cook for about 5-7 minutes, or until the mussels have opened. Discard any mussels that do not open.

6. **Finish the Dish:**
   - Stir in the lime juice and season with salt and pepper to taste.

7. **Serve:**
   - Transfer the mussels to serving bowls, spooning the curry sauce over the top. Garnish with fresh chopped cilantro and serve with lime wedges on the side.

Mussels with Creamy Mustard Sauce

Yield:
4 servings

Prep Time:
15 minutes

Cook Time:
15 minutes

Total Time:
30 minutes

Nutritional Information
(per serving):

🔥 **Calories: 330**

Total Fat: 23g
Saturated Fat: 13g
Cholesterol: 95mg
Sodium: 600mg
Total Carbohydrates: 5g
Dietary Fiber: 1g
Sugars: 1g
Protein: 22g

Ingredients:

2 pounds mussels, cleaned and debearded
2 tablespoons butter
1 small shallot, finely chopped
2 cloves garlic, minced
1 cup heavy cream
1/2 cup chicken broth
1/4 cup Dijon mustard
2 tablespoons whole grain mustard
1 tablespoon lemon juice
1 teaspoon lemon zest
Salt and pepper to taste
Fresh parsley, chopped (for garnish)
Lemon wedges (for serving)

1. **Prep the Mussels:**
   - If the mussels are not cleaned, scrub them under cold water and remove any beards.

2. **Sauté the Aromatics:**
   - In a large pot or Dutch oven, melt the butter over medium heat. Add the finely chopped shallot and sauté until translucent, about 3-4 minutes. Add the minced garlic and cook for another 1-2 minutes until fragrant.

3. **Deglaze the Pot:**
   - Pour in the chicken broth, scraping up any browned bits from the bottom of the pot. Bring to a simmer.

4. **Add the Mussels:**
   - Add the cleaned mussels to the pot. Cover and cook for about 5-7 minutes, or until the mussels have opened. Discard any mussels that do not open.

5. **Make the Creamy Mustard Sauce:**
   - Remove the mussels with a slotted spoon and set aside. Stir in the heavy cream, Dijon mustard, whole grain mustard, lemon juice, and lemon zest into the pot. Simmer for 3-5 minutes until the sauce thickens slightly. Season with salt and pepper to taste.

6. **Combine and Serve:**
   - Return the mussels to the pot and gently toss to coat them in the creamy mustard sauce.
   - Transfer the mussels to serving bowls, garnish with fresh chopped parsley, and serve with lemon wedges on the side.

Lobster and Bacon Wrapped Asparagus

Yield:
4 servings

Prep Time:
20 minutes

Cook Time:
20 minutes

Total Time:
40 minutes

Nutritional Information
(per serving):

♦ Calories: 320

Total Fat: 20g
Saturated Fat: 6g
Cholesterol: 115mg
Sodium: 720mg
Total Carbohydrates: 6g
Dietary Fiber: 3g
Sugars: 2g
Protein: 28g

Ingredients:

2 lobster tails, about 8 ounces each
1 pound asparagus, trimmed
8 slices bacon
2 tablespoons olive oil
2 cloves garlic, minced

1 tablespoon lemon juice
1 teaspoon lemon zest
Salt and pepper to taste
Fresh parsley, chopped (for garnish)
Lemon wedges (for serving)

1. **Preheat the Oven:**
   - Preheat your oven to 400°F (200°C). Line a baking sheet with parchment paper.

2. **Prepare the Lobster:**
   - Using kitchen shears, cut down the back of each lobster tail to expose the meat. Gently pull the lobster meat out and place it on top of the shell, keeping it attached at the base.

3. **Season the Lobster:**
   - Brush the lobster meat with olive oil and sprinkle with salt, pepper, lemon juice, and lemon zest.

4. **Wrap the Asparagus:**
   - Bundle the asparagus spears into groups of 3-4 spears each. Wrap each bundle with a slice of bacon, starting from the bottom and spiraling up to the top. Secure with a toothpick if needed.

5. **Bake the Asparagus:**
   - Place the bacon-wrapped asparagus bundles on the prepared baking sheet. Drizzle with a little olive oil and season with salt and pepper. Bake in the preheated oven for about 15 minutes, or until the bacon is crispy and the asparagus is tender.

6. **Cook the Lobster:**
   - While the asparagus is baking, place the lobster tails on another baking sheet and bake in the preheated oven for 10-12 minutes, or until the lobster meat is opaque and cooked through.

7. **Serve:**
   - Arrange the bacon-wrapped asparagus and lobster tails on a serving platter. Garnish with fresh chopped parsley and serve with lemon wedges on the side.

Creamy Lobster and Mushroom Casserole

Yield:
4 servings

Prep Time:
20 minutes

Cook Time:
30 minutes

Total Time:
50 minutes

Nutritional Information
(per serving):

🔥 **Calories: 450**

Total Fat: 35g
Saturated Fat: 20g
Cholesterol: 160mg
Sodium: 720mg
Total Carbohydrates: 8g
Dietary Fiber: 2g
Sugars: 4g
Protein: 27g

Ingredients:

2 lobster tails, about 8 ounces each
1 pound mushrooms, sliced
1 small onion, finely chopped
3 cloves garlic, minced
2 tablespoons butter
1 cup heavy cream
1/2 cup grated Parmesan cheese
1/2 cup shredded mozzarella cheese
1/4 cup chicken broth
2 tablespoons cream cheese
1 tablespoon Dijon mustard
1 teaspoon dried thyme
1 teaspoon paprika
Salt and pepper to taste
Fresh parsley, chopped (for garnish)

1. **Prepare the Lobster:**
   - Preheat your oven to 375°F (190°C).
   - Using kitchen shears, cut down the back of each lobster tail to expose the meat. Remove the meat from the shells and cut into bite-sized pieces.

2. **Cook the Mushrooms:**
   - In a large skillet, melt the butter over medium heat. Add the finely chopped onion and sauté until translucent, about 5 minutes.
   - Add the sliced mushrooms and cook until they release their moisture and start to brown, about 8 minutes. Add the minced garlic and cook for another 1-2 minutes until fragrant.

3. **Make the Creamy Sauce:**
   - Stir in the heavy cream, chicken broth, cream cheese, Dijon mustard, dried thyme, paprika, salt, and pepper. Cook, stirring frequently, until the sauce is smooth and slightly thickened, about 5 minutes.
   - Combine Ingredients:
   - Add the lobster meat to the skillet and gently fold it into the creamy mushroom mixture. Cook for 2-3 minutes until the lobster is just cooked through.

4. **Assemble the Casserole:** Transfer the mixture to a greased casserole dish. Sprinkle the grated Parmesan cheese and shredded mozzarella cheese evenly over the top.

5. **Bake:** Bake in the preheated oven for 12-15 minutes, or until the casserole is bubbly and the cheese is golden brown.

6. **Serve:** Remove from the oven and let it rest for a few minutes. Garnish with fresh chopped parsley before serving.

Lobster Deviled Eggs

Yield:
12 deviled eggs
(6 servings)

Prep Time:
15 minutes

Cook Time:
10 minutes

Total Time:
25 minutes

Nutritional Information
(per serving):

🔥 **Calories: 120**

Total Fat: 9g
Saturated Fat: 2g
Cholesterol: 185mg
Sodium: 250mg
Total Carbohydrates: 1g
Dietary Fiber: 0g
Sugars: 0g
Protein: 9g

Ingredients:

6 large eggs

4 ounces cooked lobster meat, finely chopped

1/4 cup mayonnaise

1 teaspoon Dijon mustard

1 teaspoon lemon juice

1/2 teaspoon lemon zest

1 tablespoon fresh chives, finely chopped (plus extra for garnish)

Salt and pepper to taste

Paprika for garnish

1. **Cook the Eggs:**
   - Place the eggs in a saucepan and cover with cold water. Bring to a boil over medium-high heat. Once boiling, cover the saucepan, remove from heat, and let sit for 10 minutes.
   - After 10 minutes, transfer the eggs to a bowl of ice water to cool. Once cooled, peel the eggs and slice them in half lengthwise.

2. **Prepare the Filling:**
   - Remove the yolks from the egg halves and place them in a medium bowl. Mash the yolks with a fork until smooth.
   - Add the finely chopped lobster meat, mayonnaise, Dijon mustard, lemon juice, lemon zest, and chopped chives to the mashed yolks. Mix until well combined. Season with salt and pepper to taste.

3. **Fill the Egg Whites:**
   - Spoon or pipe the lobster yolk mixture into the hollowed-out egg whites.

4. **Garnish and Serve:**
   - Sprinkle the deviled eggs with a little paprika and garnish with extra chopped chives.
   - Arrange the deviled eggs on a serving platter and serve immediately or refrigerate until ready to serve.

Baby Octopus Ceviche

Yield:
4 servings

Prep Time:
20 minutes

Cook Time:
5 minute
(plus 1 hour for marinating)

Total Time:
1 hour 25 minutes

Nutritional Information
(per serving):

🔥 **Calories: 180**

Total Fat: 9g
Saturated Fat: 1.5g
Cholesterol: 100mg
Sodium: 290mg
Total Carbohydrates: 10g
Dietary Fiber: 4g
Sugars: 3g
Protein: 17g

Ingredients:

1 pound baby octopus, cleaned

1/2 cup fresh lime juice (about 4-5 limes)

1/4 cup fresh lemon juice (about 2 lemons)

1/4 cup fresh orange juice (about 1 orange)

1 small red onion, finely chopped

1 jalapeño, seeded and finely chopped

1 cup cherry tomatoes, quartered

1/2 cup cucumber, finely diced

1/4 cup fresh cilantro, chopped

2 cloves garlic, minced

1 avocado, diced

1 tablespoon olive oil

Salt and pepper to taste

Lime wedges (for serving)

1. **Cook the Octopus:**
   - Bring a pot of water to a boil. Add the baby octopus and cook for 3-5 minutes until tender. Drain and let cool. Once cooled, cut the octopus into bite-sized pieces.

2. **Marinate the Octopus:**
   - In a large bowl, combine the fresh lime juice, lemon juice, and orange juice. Add the chopped octopus, finely chopped red onion, minced garlic, and chopped jalapeño. Mix well. Cover and refrigerate for at least 1 hour to allow the flavors to meld.

3. **Prepare the Vegetables:**
   - In a separate bowl, combine the quartered cherry tomatoes, finely diced cucumber, chopped fresh cilantro, and diced avocado.

4. **Combine and Serve:**
   - After the octopus has marinated, add the vegetable mixture to the bowl. Drizzle with olive oil and season with salt and pepper to taste. Toss gently to combine.
   - Serve the ceviche in individual bowls or on a platter, garnished with lime wedges.

Lobster and Cream Cheese Stuffed Peppers

Yield:
4 servings

Prep Time:
20 minutes

Cook Time:
25 minutes

Total Time:
45 minutes

Nutritional Information
(per serving):

🔥 Calories: 320

Total Fat: 24g
Saturated Fat: 12g
Cholesterol: 100mg
Sodium: 450mg
Total Carbohydrates: 10g
Dietary Fiber: 3g
Sugars: 5g
Protein: 18g

Ingredients:

4 large bell peppers (any color), halved and seeds removed

8 ounces cooked lobster meat, finely chopped

8 ounces cream cheese, softened

1/2 cup shredded mozzarella cheese

1/4 cup grated Parmesan cheese

2 cloves garlic, minced

1 small shallot, finely chopped

2 tablespoons fresh parsley, chopped (plus extra for garnish)

1 tablespoon lemon juice

1 teaspoon lemon zest

Salt and pepper to taste

2 tablespoons olive oil

1. **Preheat the Oven:**
   - Preheat your oven to 375°F (190°C). Line a baking sheet with parchment paper.

2. **Prepare the Peppers:**
   - Place the halved bell peppers on the baking sheet, cut side up. Drizzle with olive oil and season with salt and pepper. Roast in the preheated oven for 10 minutes to soften slightly.

3. **Make the Filling:**
   - In a medium bowl, combine the chopped lobster meat, softened cream cheese, shredded mozzarella cheese, grated Parmesan cheese, minced garlic, finely chopped shallot, chopped parsley, lemon juice, and lemon zest. Mix until well combined. Season with salt and pepper to taste.

4. **Stuff the Peppers:**
   - Remove the bell peppers from the oven and let cool slightly. Spoon the lobster and cream cheese mixture into each pepper half, packing the filling in tightly.

5. **Bake the Stuffed Peppers:**
   - Return the stuffed peppers to the oven and bake for 15 minutes, or until the filling is hot and the tops are golden brown.

6. **Serve:**
   - Remove from the oven and let cool for a few minutes. Garnish with extra chopped parsley before serving.

Braised Baby Octopus in Tomato Sauce

Yield:
4 servings

Prep Time:
20 minutes

Cook Time:
1 hour 15 minutes

Total Time:
1 hour 35 minutes

Nutritional Information
(per serving):

🔥 Calories: 220

Total Fat: 8g
Saturated Fat: 1.5g
Cholesterol: 180mg
Sodium: 500mg
Total Carbohydrates: 8g
Dietary Fiber: 2g
Sugars: 4g
Protein: 25g

Ingredients:

1.5 pounds baby octopus, cleaned

2 tablespoons olive oil

1 medium onion, finely chopped

3 cloves garlic, minced

1 can (14.5 ounces) diced tomatoes (no added sugar)

1/2 cup dry white wine

1/2 cup chicken broth

2 tablespoons tomato paste

1 teaspoon dried oregano

1 teaspoon dried basil

1/2 teaspoon red pepper flakes (optional)

Salt and pepper to taste

1/4 cup fresh parsley, chopped (for garnish)

1. **Prepare the Octopus:**
   - If the octopus is not cleaned, clean it thoroughly under cold water. Cut the octopus into bite-sized pieces.

2. **Sauté the Aromatics:**
   - In a large pot or Dutch oven, heat the olive oil over medium heat. Add the finely chopped onion and sauté until translucent, about 5 minutes. Add the minced garlic and cook for another 1-2 minutes until fragrant.

3. **Add the Liquids:**
   - Stir in the dry white wine, chicken broth, and tomato paste. Cook for 2-3 minutes, allowing the liquid to reduce slightly.

4. **Add the Tomatoes and Seasonings:**
   - Add the diced tomatoes, dried oregano, dried basil, and red pepper flakes (if using). Season with salt and pepper to taste. Bring the mixture to a simmer.

5. **Add the Octopus:**
   - Add the chopped octopus to the pot, stirring to combine. Cover the pot and reduce the heat to low. Simmer for 1 hour, stirring occasionally, until the octopus is tender and the sauce has thickened.

6. **Serve:**
   - Taste and adjust seasoning if necessary. Serve the braised octopus in bowls, garnished with fresh chopped parsley.

Baby Octopus Greek Salad

Yield:
4 servings

Prep Time:
20 minutes

Cook Time:
10 minutes

Total Time:
30 minutes

Nutritional Information
(per serving):

🔥 **Calories: 250**

Total Fat: 18g
Saturated Fat: 6g
Cholesterol: 180mg
Sodium: 580mg
Total Carbohydrates: 7g
Dietary Fiber: 2g
Sugars: 3g
Protein: 18g

Ingredients:

1 pound baby octopus, cleaned
1/4 cup olive oil
2 tablespoons lemon juice
1 teaspoon dried oregano
1 clove garlic, minced
Salt and pepper to taste
1 cucumber, diced

1 cup cherry tomatoes, halved
1/2 red onion, thinly sliced
1/2 cup Kalamata olives, pitted and halved
1/2 cup feta cheese, crumbled
1/4 cup fresh parsley, chopped

1. **Prepare the Octopus:**
   - If the octopus is not cleaned, clean it thoroughly under cold water. Cut the octopus into bite-sized pieces.

2. **Cook the Octopus:**
   - In a large pot, bring water to a boil. Add the octopus and cook for 3-5 minutes until tender. Drain and let cool.

3. **Marinate the Octopus:**
   - In a bowl, whisk together 2 tablespoons of olive oil, lemon juice, dried oregano, minced garlic, salt, and pepper. Add the cooled octopus and toss to coat. Let marinate for at least 10 minutes.

4. **Prepare the Salad:**
   - In a large salad bowl, combine the diced cucumber, halved cherry tomatoes, thinly sliced red onion, halved Kalamata olives, crumbled feta cheese, and chopped fresh parsley.

5. **Assemble the Salad:**
   - Add the marinated octopus to the salad bowl. Drizzle with the remaining 2 tablespoons of olive oil. Toss gently to combine all the ingredients.

6. **Serve:**
   - Serve immediately or chill in the refrigerator for 10-15 minutes before serving to allow the flavors to meld together.

Roasted Baby Octopus with Broccoli Rabe

Yield:
4 servings

Prep Time:
15 minutes

Cook Time:
30 minutes

Total Time:
45 minutes

Nutritional Information
(per serving):

🔥 **Calories: 220**

Total Fat: 14g
Saturated Fat: 2g
Cholesterol: 160mg
Sodium: 480mg
Total Carbohydrates: 6g
Dietary Fiber: 3g
Sugars: 1g
Protein: 18g

Ingredients:

1.5 pounds baby octopus, cleaned

1 large bunch broccoli rabe, trimmed and washed

4 tablespoons olive oil, divided

3 cloves garlic, minced

1 lemon, zest and juice

1 teaspoon dried oregano

1/2 teaspoon red pepper flakes (optional)

Salt and pepper to taste

Fresh parsley, chopped (for garnish)

1. **Preheat the Oven:**
   - Preheat your oven to 400°F (200°C). Line a baking sheet with parchment paper.

2. **Prepare the Octopus:**
   - If the octopus is not cleaned, clean it thoroughly under cold water. Pat the octopus dry with paper towels. Cut the octopus into bite-sized pieces.

3. **Season the Octopus:**
   - In a large bowl, combine 2 tablespoons of olive oil, minced garlic, lemon zest, dried oregano, red pepper flakes (if using), salt, and pepper. Add the octopus and toss to coat evenly.

4. **Roast the Octopus:**
   - Spread the octopus pieces in a single layer on the prepared baking sheet. Roast in the preheated oven for 20-25 minutes, or until the octopus is tender and slightly crispy on the edges.

5. **Prepare the Broccoli Rabe:**
   - While the octopus is roasting, bring a large pot of salted water to a boil. Blanch the broccoli rabe for 2-3 minutes until bright green and tender. Drain and transfer to an ice bath to stop the cooking process. Drain again and pat dry.

6. **Sauté the Broccoli Rabe:**
   - In a large skillet, heat the remaining 2 tablespoons of olive oil over medium heat. Add the blanched broccoli rabe and sauté for 3-4 minutes until heated through. Season with salt and pepper to taste.

7. **Combine and Serve:**
   - Remove the roasted octopus from the oven. In a large serving bowl or platter, combine the roasted octopus and sautéed broccoli rabe. Drizzle with lemon juice and garnish with fresh chopped parsley.

Grilled Tiger Prawns with Lemon Herb Marinade

Yield:
4 servings

Prep Time:
15 minutes
(plus 30 minutes marinating time)

Cook Time:
10 minutes

Total Time:
55 minutes

Nutritional Information
(per serving):

🔥 **Calories: 220**

Total Fat: 14g
Saturated Fat: 2g
Cholesterol: 185mg
Sodium: 380mg
Total Carbohydrates: 2g
Dietary Fiber: 0g
Sugars: 0g
Protein: 20g

Ingredients:

1.5 pounds tiger prawns, deveined and shells removed (leave tails on)

1/4 cup olive oil

2 tablespoons lemon juice

1 tablespoon lemon zest

3 cloves garlic, minced

2 tablespoons fresh parsley, chopped

1 tablespoon fresh basil, chopped

1 tablespoon fresh thyme, chopped

1 teaspoon Dijon mustard

Salt and pepper to taste

Lemon wedges (for serving)

1. **Prepare the Marinade:**
   - In a large bowl, whisk together the olive oil, lemon juice, lemon zest, minced garlic, chopped parsley, chopped basil, chopped thyme, Dijon mustard, salt, and pepper.

2. **Marinate the Prawns:**
   - Add the cleaned tiger prawns to the bowl with the marinade. Toss to coat the prawns evenly. Cover and refrigerate for at least 30 minutes.

3. **Preheat the Grill:**
   - Preheat your grill to medium-high heat.

4. **Grill the Prawns:**
   - Remove the prawns from the marinade and thread them onto skewers (if using wooden skewers, soak them in water for 30 minutes prior to use).
   - Grill the prawns for 2-3 minutes per side, or until they are opaque and cooked through. Avoid overcooking, as prawns can become tough.

5. **Serve:**
   - Transfer the grilled prawns to a serving platter. Serve with lemon wedges on the side for squeezing over the prawns.

CHAPTER 7

Keto Bread

Almond Flour Bread

Yield:
1 loaf
(12 slices)

Prep Time:
10 minutes

Cook Time:
45 minutes

Total Time:
55 minutes

Nutritional Information
(per slice):

🔥 **Calories: 190**

Protein: 7 g
Fat: 16 g
Carbohydrates: 6 g
Fiber: 3 g
Net Carbs: 3 g

Ingredients:

2 1/2 cups almond flour

1/4 cup ground flaxseed

1/2 teaspoon salt

1 tablespoon baking powder

5 large eggs

1/4 cup coconut oil, melted

1 tablespoon apple cider vinegar

1. **Preheat Oven:**
   - Preheat your oven to 350°F (175°C). Line a loaf pan with parchment paper or grease it well to prevent sticking.

2. **Mix Dry Ingredients:**
   - In a large bowl, combine the almond flour, ground flaxseed, salt, and baking powder. Mix thoroughly to combine.

3. **Add Wet Ingredients:**
   - In another bowl, whisk the eggs, melted coconut oil, and apple cider vinegar together until smooth.

4. **Combine Mixtures:**
   - Pour the wet ingredients into the dry ingredients and mix until well incorporated. The batter will be thick but pourable.

5. **Pour into Pan:**
   - Transfer the batter to the prepared loaf pan, smoothing the top with a spatula.

6. **Bake:**
   - Bake in the preheated oven for about 45 minutes, or until the top is golden brown and a toothpick inserted into the center comes out clean.

7. **Cool:**
   - Let the bread cool in the pan for 10 minutes, then transfer to a wire rack to cool completely before slicing.

Sesame Seed Bread

Yield:
1 loaf
(12 slices)

Prep Time:
10 minutes

Cook Time:
40 minutes

Total Time:
50 minutes

Nutritional Information
(per slice):

🔥 Calories: 180

Protein: 6 g
Fat: 15 g
Carbohydrates: 7 g
Fiber: 4 g
Net Carbs: 3 g

Ingredients:

2 cups almond flour

1/2 cup sesame seeds, plus extra for topping

1/4 cup psyllium husk powder

1 tablespoon baking powder

1/2 teaspoon salt

4 large eggs

1/4 cup olive oil

1/2 cup warm water

1 tablespoon apple cider vinegar

1. **Preheat Oven:**
   - Preheat your oven to 350ºF (175ºC). Line a loaf pan with parchment paper or grease it well.

2. **Mix Dry Ingredients:**
   - In a large bowl, combine the almond flour, sesame seeds, psyllium husk powder, baking powder, and salt. Stir together to distribute the ingredients evenly.

3. **Combine Wet Ingredients:**
   - In a separate bowl, whisk together the eggs, olive oil, and apple cider vinegar. Add warm water to the mixture and continue to whisk until fully combined.

4. **Form the Batter:**
   - Pour the wet ingredients into the dry ingredients. Mix until a thick dough forms. The psyllium husk will help bind the dough and give it a bread-like texture.

5. **Prepare for Baking:**
   - Transfer the dough to the prepared loaf pan. Smooth the top with a spatula and sprinkle additional sesame seeds over the top.

6. **Bake:**
   - Place in the preheated oven and bake for about 40 minutes, or until the bread has risen and the top is golden brown. A toothpick inserted into the center should come out clean.

7. **Cool:**
   - Remove the bread from the oven and let it cool in the pan for 10 minutes. Then, transfer it to a wire rack to cool completely before slicing.

Pizza Base

Yield:
1 pizza crust
(8 slices)

Prep Time:
10 minutes

Cook Time:
20 minutes

Total Time:
30 minutes

Nutritional Information
(per slice, crust only):

🔥 **Calories: 130**

Protein: 4 g
Fat: 10 g
Carbohydrates: 5 g
Fiber: 3 g
Net Carbs: 2 g

Ingredients:

1 cup almond flour

1/4 cup coconut flour

2 tablespoons psyllium husk powder

1 teaspoon baking powder

1/2 teaspoon salt

1 teaspoon Italian seasoning (optional)

1 teaspoon garlic powder (optional)

2 large eggs

2 tablespoons olive oil

1/2 cup warm water

1. **Preheat Oven:**
   - Preheat your oven to 350°F (175°C). Line a baking sheet or pizza stone with parchment paper.

2. **Mix Dry Ingredients:**
   - In a large bowl, combine almond flour, coconut flour, psyllium husk powder, baking powder, salt, Italian seasoning, and garlic powder. Mix well to distribute evenly.

3. **Add Wet Ingredients:**
   - In a separate bowl, whisk together the eggs and olive oil. Add this mixture to the dry ingredients, and start to mix. Gradually add the warm water while stirring until a dough forms. The dough should be pliable and hold together, but not sticky.

4. **Form the Crust:**
   - Place the dough on the parchment-lined baking sheet or pizza stone. Using your hands, press the dough out into a circle or rectangle, about 1/4 inch thick. Use a rolling pin if necessary to even it out.

5. **Pre-Bake the Crust:**
   - Bake the crust in the preheated oven for about 10-12 minutes, or until it begins to turn golden brown and feels firm to the touch.

6. **Add Toppings:**
   - Remove the crust from the oven and add your favorite low-carb pizza toppings.

7. **Final Bake:**
   - Return the pizza to the oven and bake for an additional 8-10 minutes, or until the toppings are hot and the cheese is bubbly.

8. **Serve:**
   - Let the pizza cool for a few minutes before slicing and serving.

Keto Buns

Yield:
6 buns

Prep Time:
15 minutes

Cook Time:
20 minutes

Total Time:
35 minutes

Nutritional Information
(per bun):

🔥 **Calories: 180**

Protein: 6 g
Fat: 15 g
Carbohydrates: 8 g
Fiber: 5 g
Net Carbs: 3 g

Ingredients:

1 1/2 cups almond flour

5 tablespoons ground psyllium husk powder

2 teaspoons baking powder

1 teaspoon sea salt

2 teaspoons apple cider vinegar

1 cup boiling water

3 egg whites

2 tablespoons sesame seeds (optional, for topping)

1. **Preheat Oven:**
   - Preheat your oven to 350°F (175°C). Line a baking sheet with parchment paper.

2. **Mix Dry Ingredients:**
   - In a large bowl, combine the almond flour, psyllium husk powder, baking powder, and sea salt.

3. **Add Wet Ingredients:**
   - Add the egg whites and apple cider vinegar to the dry ingredients. Mix until well combined.

4. **Boil Water:**
   - Bring water to a boil.

5. **Combine with Boiling Water:**
   - Add the boiling water to the mixture while beating with a hand mixer for about 30 seconds. Don't overmix the dough; the consistency should resemble Play-Doh.

6. **Form Buns:**
   - Moisten hands and form six pieces of dough into rounds. Place on the prepared baking sheet. Sprinkle with sesame seeds on top if desired.

7. **Bake:**
   - Bake on the lower rack in the oven for about 50-60 minutes, depending on the size of your buns. They should be firm and sound hollow when tapped.

8. **Cool:**
   - Let the buns cool completely on a rack. They will continue to firm up as they cool.

Coconut Flour Bread

Yield:
1 loaf
(12 slices)

Prep Time:
15 minutes

Cook Time:
45 minutes

Total Time:
1 hour

Nutritional Information
(per slice):

🔥 **Calories: 155**

Protein: 4 g
Fat: 12 g
Carbohydrates: 5 g
Fiber: 3 g
Net Carbs: 2 g

Ingredients:

3/4 cup coconut flour

1/2 cup melted butter (or coconut oil for a dairy-free option)

6 large eggs

1 tablespoon baking powder

1/4 teaspoon sea salt

Optional: 1 tablespoon erythritol or preferred sweetener

1. **Preheat Oven:**
   - Preheat your oven to 350°F (175°C). Line a loaf pan with parchment paper or grease it well.

2. **Combine Dry Ingredients:**
   - In a large bowl, sift together the coconut flour, baking powder, and salt.

3. **Mix Wet Ingredients:**
   - In a separate bowl, whisk together the eggs, melted butter, and erythritol (if using) until well blended.

4. **Combine Mixtures:**
   - Gradually add the wet ingredients to the dry ingredients, stirring until there are no lumps. Coconut flour is highly absorbent, so ensure all ingredients are well incorporated.

5. **Prepare the Loaf:**
   - Pour the batter into the prepared loaf pan, smoothing the top with a spatula.

6. **Bake:**
   - Bake in the preheated oven for about 45 minutes, or until the top is golden brown and a toothpick inserted into the center comes out clean.

7. **Cool:**
   - Allow the bread to cool in the pan for about 10 minutes before removing it. Transfer to a wire rack to cool completely before slicing.

Cheesy Garlic Bread

Yield:
8 servings

Prep Time:
10 minutes

Cook Time:
15 minutes

Total Time:
25 minutes

Nutritional Information
(per serving):

🔥 Calories: 210

Protein: 9 g
Fat: 18 g
Carbohydrates: 3 g
Fiber: 1 g
Net Carbs: 2 g

Ingredients:

1 1/2 cups shredded mozzarella cheese

2/3 cup almond flour

2 tablespoons cream cheese

1 large egg

1 teaspoon garlic powder

1/2 teaspoon salt

1/4 cup grated Parmesan cheese

1/4 cup shredded cheddar cheese

2 tablespoons butter, melted

2 cloves garlic, minced

1 tablespoon fresh parsley, chopped

1. **Preheat Oven:** Preheat your oven to 375°F (190°C). Line a baking sheet with parchment paper or a silicone mat.

2. **Make the Dough:** In a microwave-safe bowl, combine mozzarella and cream cheese. Microwave for 1 minute, stir, and then microwave for another 30 seconds until fully melted. Stir again to mix well.

3. **Add Dry Ingredients:** To the melted cheese mixture, add the almond flour, garlic powder, and salt. Mix until combined.

4. **Add Egg:** Stir in the egg, mixing thoroughly until the dough is uniform.

5. **Shape the Bread:** Place the dough on the prepared baking sheet, and use your hands or a rolling pin to flatten it into a rectangle about 1/2 inch thick.

6. **Add Toppings:** Brush the top of the dough with melted butter mixed with minced garlic. Sprinkle with Parmesan cheese and cheddar cheese.

7. **Bake:** Bake in the preheated oven for 15-17 minutes, or until the cheese is bubbly and slightly golden.

8. **Garnish:** Once done, sprinkle chopped parsley over the top for freshness.

9. **Serve:** Cut into strips and serve warm.

Bagels

Yield:
6 bagels

Prep Time:
15 minutes

Cook Time:
12-14 minutes

Total Time:
About 30 minutes

Nutritional Information
(per bagel):

🔥 **Calories: 330**

Protein: 18 g
Fat: 26 g
Carbohydrates: 7 g
Fiber: 3 g
Net Carbs: 4 g

Ingredients:

1 1/2 cups almond flour

1/4 cup coconut flour

2 teaspoons baking powder

1 teaspoon garlic powder (optional, for flavor)

1 teaspoon onion powder (optional, for flavor)

2 1/2 cups shredded mozzarella cheese

2 ounces cream cheese

2 large eggs

Sesame seeds, poppy seeds, or everything bagel seasoning (for topping)

1. **Preheat Oven:** Preheat your oven to 400°F (200°C). Line a baking sheet with parchment paper or a silicone baking mat.

2. **Mix Dry Ingredients:** In a medium bowl, whisk together the almond flour, coconut flour, baking powder, garlic powder, and onion powder.

3. **Melt Cheese:** In a large microwave-safe bowl, add the mozzarella and cream cheese. Microwave on high for about 90 seconds, stirring halfway through until the cheese is completely melted and easy to stir.

4. **Add Eggs:** Stir the eggs into the melted cheese mixture until well combined. It helps to do this quickly before the cheese starts to harden.

5. **Combine with Dry Ingredients:**
   • Add the dry ingredients to the cheese and egg mixture, mixing until a dough forms. If the dough becomes too hard to mix, you can reheat it briefly in the microwave.

6. **Form Bagels:** Divide the dough into 6 equal portions. Roll each portion into a ball, then press a hole in the center to form a bagel shape. Place on the prepared baking sheet.

7. **Add Toppings:** Sprinkle the bagels with sesame seeds, poppy seeds, or everything bagel seasoning, pressing lightly to adhere.

8. **Bake:** Bake in the preheated oven for 12-14 minutes, or until golden and firm.

9. **Cool:** Let the bagels cool on the baking sheet for about 10 minutes, then move them to a wire rack to cool completely.

Zucchini Bread

Yield:
1 loaf
(12 slices)

Prep Time:
15 minutes

Cook Time:
50 minutes

Total Time:
1 hour 5 minutes

Nutritional Information
(per slice):

🔥 Calories: 150

Protein: 5 g
Fat: 12 g
Carbohydrates: 6 g
Fiber: 3 g
Net Carbs: 3 g

Ingredients:

1 1/2 cups almond flour

1/2 cup coconut flour

1/4 cup erythritol (or another keto-friendly sweetener)

2 teaspoons cinnamon

1/2 teaspoon nutmeg

1 teaspoon baking powder

1/2 teaspoon salt

3 large eggs

1/4 cup unsalted butter, melted

1 teaspoon vanilla extract

1 cup grated zucchini (water squeezed out)

Optional: 1/2 cup chopped walnuts or pecans

1. **Preheat Oven:** Preheat your oven to 350°F (175°C). Line a loaf pan with parchment paper or grease it well.

2. **Prepare Zucchini:** Grate the zucchini and use a clean cloth or paper towels to squeeze out as much water as possible. This is important to prevent the bread from becoming too soggy.

3. **Mix Dry Ingredients:** In a large bowl, whisk together the almond flour, coconut flour, erythritol, cinnamon, nutmeg, baking powder, and salt.

4. **Combine Wet Ingredients:** In a separate bowl, beat the eggs with the melted butter and vanilla extract until well combined.

5. **Combine All Ingredients:** Add the wet ingredients to the dry ingredients and stir until just combined. Fold in the grated zucchini and optional nuts, if using.

6. **Pour into Pan:** Transfer the batter to the prepared loaf pan, smoothing the top with a spatula.

7. **Bake:** Bake in the preheated oven for about 50 minutes, or until a toothpick inserted into the center comes out clean.

8. **Cool:** Let the bread cool in the pan for about 10 minutes, then transfer to a wire rack to cool completely.

Cinnamon Swirl Bread

Yield:
1 loaf
(12 slices)

Prep Time:
20 minutes

Cook Time:
45 minutes

Total Time:
1 hour 5 minutes

Nutritional Information
(per slice):

🔥 **Calories: 220**

Protein: 6 g
Fat: 20 g
Carbohydrates: 5 g
Fiber: 3 g
Net Carbs: 2 g

Ingredients:

Bread:
2 cups almond flour
1/4 cup coconut flour
1/3 cup erythritol
2 teaspoons baking powder
1/2 teaspoon salt
1/2 cup unsalted butter, melted

4 large eggs
1/2 cup unsweetened almond milk
1 teaspoon vanilla extract
Cinnamon Swirl:
1/4 cup erythritol
2 tablespoons ground cinnamon
2 tablespoons melted butter

1. **Preheat Oven:** Preheat your oven to 350°F (175°C). Line a loaf pan with parchment paper, or grease it well.

2. **Prepare Dry Ingredients:** In a large bowl, combine almond flour, coconut flour, erythritol, baking powder, and salt.

3. **Mix Wet Ingredients:** In a separate bowl, whisk together the melted butter, eggs, almond milk, and vanilla extract.

4. **Combine Mixtures:** Gradually add the wet ingredients to the dry ingredients, stirring until well combined.

5. **Make Cinnamon Swirl Mixture:** In a small bowl, mix the erythritol, ground cinnamon, and melted butter for the swirl.

6. **Assemble the Bread:** Pour half of the bread batter into the prepared loaf pan. Then, sprinkle half of the cinnamon swirl mixture over the batter. Pour the remaining batter on top, and finish with the remaining cinnamon swirl mixture. Use a knife or a skewer to swirl the cinnamon mixture into the batter.

7. **Bake:** Place the pan in the oven and bake for about 45 minutes, or until a toothpick inserted into the center of the bread comes out clean.

8. **Cool:** Allow the bread to cool in the pan for about 10 minutes before transferring it to a wire rack to cool completely.

Olive Bread

Yield:
1 loaf
(12 slices)

Prep Time:
15 minutes

Cook Time:
40 minutes

Total Time:
55 minutes

Nutritional Information
(per slice):

🔥 **Calories: 210**

Protein: 7 g
Fat: 18 g
Carbohydrates: 6 g
Fiber: 3 g
Net Carbs: 3 g

Ingredients:

2 cups almond flour

1/3 cup coconut flour

1 tablespoon baking powder

1/2 teaspoon salt

1 teaspoon garlic powder (optional, for extra flavor)

5 large eggs

1/2 cup sour cream

1/4 cup olive oil

1 cup pitted and chopped Kalamata olives

1/2 cup grated Parmesan cheese

1 tablespoon fresh rosemary, chopped (or 1 teaspoon dried rosemary)

1. **Preheat Oven:** Preheat your oven to 350°F (175°C). Line a loaf pan with parchment paper or grease it well.

2. **Mix Dry Ingredients:** In a large bowl, whisk together almond flour, coconut flour, baking powder, salt, and garlic powder if using.

3. **Whisk Wet Ingredients:** In another bowl, beat the eggs, sour cream, and olive oil until smooth.

4. **Combine:** Add the wet ingredients to the dry ingredients, mixing until just combined. Fold in the chopped olives, grated Parmesan, and rosemary.

5. **Pour into Pan:** Transfer the batter to the prepared loaf pan and smooth the top with a spatula.

6. **Bake:** Bake in the preheated oven for about 40 minutes, or until the top is golden brown and a toothpick inserted into the center comes out clean.

7. **Cool:** Let the bread cool in the pan for 10 minutes, then transfer it to a wire rack to cool completely.

CHAPTER 8

Sweets & Desserts

Cheesecake

Yield:
12 servings

Prep Time:
20 minutes

Cook Time:
50 minutes

Total Time:
1 hour 10 minutes +
chilling time

Nutritional Information
(per serving):

🔥 **Calories: 310**

Protein: 6 g
Fat: 29 g
Carbohydrates: 4 g
Fiber: 1 g
Net Carbs: 3 g

Ingredients:

For the crust:

1 1/2 cups almond flour
1/4 cup erythritol
1 teaspoon vanilla extract
1/3 cup unsalted butter, melted

For the filling:

24 ounces cream cheese, softened
1 cup erythritol
1 cup sour cream
3 large eggs
1 tablespoon lemon juice
1 teaspoon vanilla extract

1. **Prepare the Crust:**
   - Preheat your oven to 350°F (175°C).
   - Combine almond flour, erythritol, and vanilla extract in a bowl. Add melted butter and mix until a dough forms.
   - Press the dough into the bottom of a 9-inch springform pan, forming a slight edge around the sides. Bake for about 10 minutes until golden and set. Remove from the oven and let cool.

2. **Make the Filling:**
   - In a large mixing bowl, beat the softened cream cheese and erythritol until smooth and creamy.
   - Mix in sour cream, then add eggs one at a time, mixing on low after each just until blended. Stir in lemon juice and vanilla extract.

3. **Assemble and Bake:**
   - Pour the filling into the cooled crust.
   - Bake in the preheated oven for about 40 minutes. The center should be slightly jiggly, but the edges should be set.
   - Turn off the oven and leave the door slightly open to let the cheesecake cool slowly for 1 hour. This helps prevent cracking.

4. **Chill:**
   - After cooling in the oven, remove the cheesecake and chill in the refrigerator for at least 4 hours, preferably overnight.

5. **Serve:**
   - Once chilled, remove the cheesecake from the springform pan, slice, and serve.

Chocolate Mousse

Yield:
4 servings

Prep Time:
15 minutes

Cook Time:
0 minutes
(chill for at least
1 hour)

Total Time:
1 hour 15 minutes

Nutritional Information
(per serving):

🔥 **Calories: 290**

Protein: 2 g
Fat: 29 g
Carbohydrates: 5 g
Fiber: 2 g
Net Carbs: 3 g

Ingredients:

1 1/2 cups heavy whipping cream

1/4 cup unsweetened cocoa powder

1/4 cup erythritol (powdered for smoother texture)

1 teaspoon vanilla extract

Optional: a pinch of salt to enhance flavor

1. **Chill Mixing Bowl:**
   - Begin by chilling your mixing bowl and beaters in the freezer for about 10 minutes. This helps the cream whip up more easily.

2. **Whip Heavy Cream:**
   - Remove the bowl and beaters from the freezer. Pour the heavy whipping cream into the bowl and whip on high speed until soft peaks form.

3. **Add Ingredients:**
   - Reduce the mixer's speed and gradually add the unsweetened cocoa powder, erythritol, vanilla extract, and a pinch of salt if using. Increase the speed back to high and continue to whip until stiff peaks form. Be careful not to overbeat.

4. **Chill:**
   - Spoon the mousse into serving dishes. For best results, cover and refrigerate for at least one hour to set the mousse and develop the flavors.

5. **Serve:**
   - Serve chilled, optionally topping with a sprinkle of cocoa powder, a few berries, or a dollop of whipped cream for an extra special touch.

Brownies

Yield:
16 brownies

Prep Time:
10 minutes

Cook Time:
20 minutes

Total Time:
30 minutes

Nutritional Information
(per brownie):

🔥 **Calories: 110**

Protein: 3 g
Fat: 10 g
Carbohydrates: 3 g
Fiber: 1 g
Net Carbs: 2 g

Ingredients:

1/2 cup almond flour

1/3 cup cocoa powder, unsweetened

3/4 cup erythritol (or another keto-friendly sweetener)

1/2 teaspoon baking powder

1/4 teaspoon salt

3 large eggs

1/2 cup unsalted butter, melted

1 teaspoon vanilla extract

Optional: 1/2 cup sugar-free chocolate chips or nuts (like walnuts or pecans)

1. **Preheat Oven and Prepare Pan:**
   - Preheat your oven to 350°F (175°C). Line an 8x8 inch baking pan with parchment paper, leaving some overhang for easy removal.

2. **Mix Dry Ingredients:**
   - In a medium bowl, whisk together the almond flour, cocoa powder, erythritol, baking powder, and salt.

3. **Combine Wet Ingredients:**
   - In another bowl, beat the eggs with the melted butter and vanilla extract until well combined.

4. **Combine Wet and Dry Ingredients:**
   - Gradually mix the wet ingredients into the dry ingredients until the batter is smooth. If using, fold in sugar-free chocolate chips or nuts.

5. **Pour and Smooth Batter:**
   - Pour the batter into the prepared pan and smooth the top with a spatula.

6. **Bake:**
   - Place the pan in the oven and bake for about 20 minutes, or until the edges are set but the center is still slightly soft. This will ensure the brownies are fudgy.

7. **Cool:**
   - Allow the brownies to cool completely in the pan set on a wire rack. Once cooled, lift out using the parchment paper and cut into squares.

Lemon Bars

Yield:
16 bars

Prep Time:
15 minutes

Cook Time:
25 minutes

Total Time:
40 minutes

Nutritional Information
(per bar):

🔥 **Calories: 110**

Protein: 3 g
Fat: 9 g
Carbohydrates: 3 g
Fiber: 1 g
Net Carbs: 2 g

Ingredients:

For the crust:

1 1/2 cups almond flour

1/4 cup erythritol (or another keto-friendly sweetener)

1/4 teaspoon salt

1/3 cup unsalted butter, melted

For the filling:

3/4 cup lemon juice (about 4-5 lemons)

Zest of 2 lemons

1/2 cup erythritol

4 large eggs

2 tablespoons almond flour

Powdered erythritol, for dusting (optional, for garnish)

1. **Preheat Oven and Prepare Pan:**
   - Preheat your oven to 350°F (175°C). Line an 8x8 inch baking pan with parchment paper, leaving some overhang for easy removal.

2. **Make the Crust:**
   - In a mixing bowl, combine almond flour, erythritol, and salt. Stir in melted butter until well combined. Press the mixture evenly into the bottom of the prepared pan.

3. **Bake the Crust:**
   - Bake the crust in the preheated oven for about 10-12 minutes, or until lightly golden. Remove from the oven and set aside.

4. **Make the Filling:**
   - In a separate bowl, whisk together lemon juice, lemon zest, erythritol, eggs, and almond flour until smooth.

5. **Pour Filling Over Crust:**
   - Pour the lemon filling over the pre-baked crust, spreading it out evenly.

6. **Bake the Bars:**
   - Return the pan to the oven and bake for another 15-18 minutes, or until the filling is set and no longer jiggles.

7. **Cool and Chill:**
   - Allow the bars to cool completely in the pan on a wire rack. Once cooled, transfer to the refrigerator and chill for at least 2 hours, or until firm.

8. **Slice and Serve:**
   - Once chilled, lift the bars out of the pan using the parchment paper overhang. Dust with powdered erythritol if desired, then slice into squares and serve.

Peanut Butter Cookies

Yield:
24 cookies

Prep Time:
10 minutes

Cook Time:
12 minutes

Total Time:
22 minutes

Nutritional Information
(per cookie):

🔥 **Calories: 80**

Protein: 3 g
Fat: 6 g
Carbohydrates: 2 g
Fiber: 1 g
Net Carbs: 1 g

Ingredients:

1 cup natural peanut butter (unsweetened and unsalted)

1/3 cup erythritol (or other keto-friendly sweetener)

1 large egg

1 teaspoon vanilla extract

1/2 teaspoon baking soda

Optional: 1/4 cup sugar-free chocolate chips or chopped nuts

1. **Preheat Oven and Prepare Baking Sheet:**
   - Preheat your oven to 350°F (175°C). Line a baking sheet with parchment paper.

2. **Mix Ingredients:**
   - In a mixing bowl, combine the peanut butter, erythritol, egg, vanilla extract, and baking soda. Stir until all ingredients are well combined. If desired, fold in sugar-free chocolate chips or chopped nuts for added texture and flavor.

3. **Shape Cookies:**
   - Using a tablespoon or cookie scoop, drop spoonfuls of the dough onto the prepared baking sheet. Press down slightly with the back of a spoon or a fork to flatten them into rounds, making a crisscross pattern on top if desired.

4. **Bake:**
   - Place in the oven and bake for 12 minutes or until the edges are slightly golden.

5. **Cool:**
   - Remove the cookies from the oven and let them cool on the baking sheet for 10 minutes before transferring them to a wire rack to cool completely.

Tiramisu

Yield:
8 servings

Prep Time:
30 minutes

Cook Time:
0 minutes
(requires about
4 hours to chill)

Total Time:
**4 hours
30 minutes**

**Nutritional
Information**
(per serving):

🔥 **Calories: 320**

Protein: 8 g
Fat: 28 g
Carbohydrates: 5 g
Fiber: 2 g
Net Carbs: 3 g

Ingredients:

For the keto ladyfingers:
1 cup almond flour
1/3 cup erythritol
4 large eggs, separated
1/2 teaspoon cream of tartar
1 teaspoon vanilla extract

For the filling:
1 1/2 cups mascarpone cheese

1/2 cup heavy cream
1/4 cup powdered erythritol
1 teaspoon vanilla extract

For the coffee layer:
1 cup strong brewed coffee, cooled
1 tablespoon rum or brandy (optional)

For dusting:
Unsweetened cocoa powder

1. **Make Keto Ladyfingers:**
   - Preheat oven to 350°F (175°C). Line a baking sheet with parchment paper.
   - In a large bowl, beat egg whites and cream of tartar until stiff peaks form. In another bowl, whisk egg yolks with erythritol and vanilla until smooth.
   - Gently fold the egg yolk mixture into the egg whites. Sift almond flour over the mixture and fold gently until combined.
   - Spoon the batter into a piping bag and pipe into long strips on the prepared baking sheet.
   - Bake for 15-18 minutes, until golden. Let cool completely.

2. **Prepare the Filling:** In a mixing bowl, combine mascarpone, heavy cream, powdered erythritol, and vanilla extract. Beat until the mixture is smooth and creamy.

3. **Assemble the Tiramisu:**
   - Cut the keto ladyfingers to fit the size of a small glass dish or individual serving cups.
   - Dip each piece briefly into the cooled coffee mixed with rum or brandy, if using, and layer them at the bottom of the dish.
   - Spread half of the mascarpone mixture over the ladyfingers. Repeat with another layer of dipped ladyfingers and finish with a layer of mascarpone mixture.
   - Cover and refrigerate for at least 4 hours, or overnight, to allow flavors to meld.

4. **Serve:** Before serving, dust the top with unsweetened cocoa powder.

Coconut Flour Pancakes

Yield:
8 pancakes

Prep Time:
10 minutes

Cook Time:
10 minutes

Total Time:
20 minutes

Nutritional Information
(per pancake):

🔥 **Calories: 105**

Protein: 3 g
Fat: 7 g
Carbohydrates: 4 g
Fiber: 2 g
Net Carbs: 2 g

Ingredients:

1/3 cup coconut flour

1 tablespoon erythritol (or other keto-friendly sweetener)

1/2 teaspoon baking powder

1/4 teaspoon salt

4 large eggs

1/4 cup unsweetened almond milk (or any keto-friendly milk)

2 tablespoons unsalted butter, melted (plus more for frying)

1/2 teaspoon vanilla extract

1. **Mix Dry Ingredients:**
   - In a large bowl, combine coconut flour, erythritol, baking powder, and salt.

2. **Whisk Wet Ingredients:**
   - In another bowl, whisk together eggs, almond milk, melted butter, and vanilla extract until well blended.

3. **Combine Mixtures:**
   - Pour the wet ingredients into the dry ingredients and stir until you have a smooth batter. Let the batter sit for a few minutes to thicken, as coconut flour absorbs more liquid than other flours.

4. **Heat a Skillet:**
   - Heat a non-stick skillet or griddle over medium heat and brush with a little butter to prevent sticking.

5. **Cook Pancakes:**
   - Pour about 1/4 cup of batter for each pancake onto the hot skillet. Cook for about 2-3 minutes on one side, or until bubbles form on the surface and the edges appear set. Flip carefully and cook for another 2-3 minutes on the other side until golden brown and cooked through.

6. **Serve Warm:**
   - Serve the pancakes warm with your choice of keto-friendly toppings such as butter, sugar-free syrup, or fresh berries.

Ice Cream

Yield:
About 6 servings

Prep Time:
10 minutes

Cook Time:
0 minutes
(plus at least
4 hours freezing
time)

Total Time:
4 hours 10 minutes

Nutritional Information
(per serving):

🔥 **Calories: 300**

Protein: 2 g
Fat: 30 g
Carbohydrates: 3 g
Fiber: 0 g
Net Carbs: 3 g

Ingredients:

2 cups heavy whipping cream

1 cup unsweetened almond milk

2/3 cup erythritol (powdered for better dissolving)

1 tablespoon pure vanilla extract

1/4 teaspoon salt

Optional: Add-ins such as keto-friendly chocolate chips, nuts, or berry puree

1. **Mix Ingredients:**
   - In a large bowl, combine the heavy cream, almond milk, erythritol, vanilla extract, and salt. Whisk everything together until the erythritol is fully dissolved and the mixture is smooth.

2. **Chill Mixture:**
   - Chill the mixture in the refrigerator for at least 1 hour to ensure it is completely cold. This step helps in achieving a smoother texture in the final product.

3. **Churn Ice Cream:**
   - Pour the chilled mixture into an ice cream maker and churn according to the manufacturer's instructions, usually about 20-25 minutes.

4. **Add Optional Ingredients:**
   - If you are adding chocolate chips, nuts, or berry puree, fold them into the mixture during the last few minutes of churning.

5. **Freeze:**
   - Transfer the churned ice cream to an airtight container and freeze for at least 3 hours, or until firm.

6. **Serve:**
   - Remove the ice cream from the freezer about 10 minutes before serving to allow it to soften slightly for easier scooping.

Chocolate Cake

Yield:
12 servings

Prep Time:
15 minutes

Cook Time:
25 minutes

Total Time:
40 minutes

Nutritional Information
(per serving):

🔥 **Calories: 320**

Protein: 7 g
Fat: 29 g
Carbohydrates: 8 g
Fiber: 4 g
Net Carbs: 4 g

Ingredients:

2 cups almond flour

3/4 cup cocoa powder, unsweetened

1/2 cup coconut flour

1 1/2 teaspoons baking powder

1 teaspoon baking soda

1/2 teaspoon salt

1 cup erythritol (granular)

4 large eggs

1 cup unsweetened almond milk

1/2 cup butter, melted

2 teaspoons vanilla extract

For the frosting:

1 cup heavy cream

1/2 cup unsweetened cocoa powder

1/3 cup erythritol (powdered)

1 teaspoon vanilla extract

1. **Preheat Oven and Prepare Pans:** Preheat your oven to 350ºF (175ºC) Grease two 8-inch round cake pans and line the bottoms with parchment paper to ensure easy removal.

2. **Mix Dry Ingredients:** In a large bowl, sift together almond flour, cocoa powder, coconut flour, baking powder, baking soda, and salt. Stir in granular erythritol.

3. **Combine Wet Ingredients:** In another bowl, whisk together eggs, almond milk, melted butter, and vanilla extract.

4. **Combine Mixtures:** Gradually mix the wet ingredients into the dry ingredients until well combined and smooth.

5. **Bake:** Divide the batter evenly between the prepared pans. Smooth the tops with a spatula. Bake for 25 minutes, or until a toothpick inserted into the center comes out clean.

6. **Cool:** Remove from the oven and allow to cool in the pans for 10 minutes, then turn out onto wire racks to cool completely.

7. **Make Frosting:** While the cakes cool, whip the heavy cream, cocoa powder, powdered erythritol, and vanilla extract together until thick and creamy.

8. **Assemble Cake:** Once the cakes are completely cool, spread frosting on the top of one cake layer. Place the second layer on top, and spread the remaining frosting over the top and sides of the cake.

Pumpkin Pie

Yield:
8 servings

Prep Time:
20 minutes

Cook Time:
45 minutes

Total Time:
1 hour 5 minutes

Nutritional Information
(per serving):

🔥 **Calories: 320**

Protein: 7 g
Fat: 29 g
Carbohydrates: 8 g
Fiber: 3 g
Net Carbs: 5 g

Ingredients:

For the crust:
1 1/2 cups almond flour
1/4 cup coconut flour
1/4 cup erythritol (granular)
1/4 teaspoon salt
6 tablespoons butter, cold and diced
1 egg

For the filling:
1 can (15 oz) pumpkin puree
3/4 cup heavy cream
1/2 cup erythritol (granular)
2 eggs
1 teaspoon vanilla extract
2 teaspoons pumpkin pie spice
1/4 teaspoon salt

1. **Prepare the Crust:**
   - Preheat oven to 350°F (175°C).
   - In a food processor, combine almond flour, coconut flour, erythritol, and salt. Pulse to mix.
   - Add cold, diced butter and pulse until mixture resembles coarse crumbs.
   - Beat the egg and add it to the processor, pulsing until a dough forms.
   - Press the dough into a 9-inch pie pan, forming an even layer along the bottom and sides.
   - Prick the bottom with a fork and pre-bake for 10 minutes. Remove from oven and set aside.

2. **Make the Filling:**
   - In a large mixing bowl, whisk together pumpkin puree, heavy cream, erythritol, eggs, vanilla extract, pumpkin pie spice, and salt until smooth.

3. **Assemble and Bake:**
   - Pour the pumpkin filling into the pre-baked crust.
   - Return to the oven and bake for 35-45 minutes, or until the filling is set and a knife inserted near the center comes out clean.

4. **Cool and Serve:**
   - Let the pie cool completely on a wire rack. Chill in the refrigerator for at least 2 hours before serving to allow the filling to set fully.
   - Serve with a dollop of whipped cream if desired.

Vanilla Cupcakes

Yield:
12 cupcakes

Prep Time:
15 minutes

Cook Time:
20 minutes

Total Time:
35 minutes

Nutritional Information
(per cupcake, including frosting):

🔥 **Calories: 280**

Protein: 6 g
Fat: 25 g
Carbohydrates: 5 g
Fiber: 2 g
Net Carbs: 3 g

Ingredients:

For the cupcakes:
1 1/2 cups almond flour
1/2 cup erythritol (granular)
1/4 cup coconut flour
2 teaspoons baking powder
1/4 teaspoon salt
6 tablespoons butter, softened
4 large eggs

1/3 cup unsweetened almond milk
2 teaspoons vanilla extract

For the frosting:
1 cup heavy cream
1/2 cup cream cheese, softened
1/4 cup erythritol (powdered)
1 teaspoon vanilla extract

1. **Prepare the Cupcakes:**
   - Preheat the oven to 350°F (175°C). Line a muffin tin with cupcake liners or grease the cups.
   - In a large bowl, mix together almond flour, erythritol, coconut flour, baking powder, and salt.
   - In another bowl, beat the softened butter with eggs, almond milk, and vanilla extract until smooth.
   - Gradually add the dry ingredients to the wet ingredients, stirring until well combined.
   - Divide the batter evenly among the 12 cupcake molds, filling each about 2/3 full.
   - Bake for 20 minutes, or until a toothpick inserted into the center of a cupcake comes out clean.

2. **Make the Frosting:**
   - While the cupcakes cool, whip the heavy cream until it begins to thicken.
   - Add softened cream cheese, powdered erythritol, and vanilla extract. Continue to whip until the mixture is smooth and creamy.
   - Chill the frosting in the refrigerator until the cupcakes are completely cool.

3. **Decorate the Cupcakes:**
   - Once cupcakes are cool, use a piping bag or a spoon to apply the frosting to the cupcakes.
   - Optionally, top with a sprinkle of keto-friendly sprinkles or a dusting of powdered erythritol.

Pecan Pie

Yield:
8 servings

Prep Time:
20 minutes

Cook Time:
45 minutes

Total Time:
1 hour 5 minutes

Nutritional Information
(per serving):

🔥 **Calories: 420**

Protein: 8 g
Fat: 40 g
Carbohydrates: 6 g
Fiber: 3 g
Net Carbs: 3 g

Ingredients:

For the crust:
1 1/2 cups almond flour
1/4 cup coconut flour
1/4 cup erythritol (granular)
1/4 teaspoon salt
6 tablespoons butter, cold and diced
1 egg

For the filling:
1 cup pecans, halved
3 large eggs
1 cup erythritol (granular)
1/2 cup butter, melted
1 teaspoon vanilla extract
1/2 cup sugar-free maple syrup or keto-friendly syrup

1. **Prepare the Crust:**
   - Preheat oven to 350°F (175°C).
   - In a food processor, blend almond flour, coconut flour, erythritol, and salt. Add cold, diced butter and pulse until the mixture resembles coarse crumbs.
   - Add the egg and pulse until a dough forms.
   - Press the dough into a 9-inch pie pan, forming an even layer along the bottom and sides.
   - Prick the bottom with a fork and pre-bake for 10 minutes. Remove from oven and set aside.

2. **Prepare the Filling:**
   - In a large mixing bowl, whisk together eggs, erythritol, melted butter, vanilla extract, and sugar-free maple syrup until well combined.
   - Stir in the pecan halves and pour the mixture into the pre-baked crust.

3. **Bake the Pie:**
   - Place the pie in the oven and bake for 35-45 minutes, or until the filling is set and the crust is golden brown.
   - If the edges of the crust begin to brown too quickly, cover them with foil during the last 15 minutes of baking.

4. **Cool and Serve:**
   - Allow the pie to cool completely on a wire rack before serving. This helps the filling set properly and makes slicing easier.

Crème Brûlée

Yield:
4 servings

Prep Time:
10 minutes

Cook Time:
40 minutes

Total Time:
50 minutes
(plus chilling
time)

**Nutritional
Information**
(per serving):

🔥 **Calories:**
440

Protein: 5 g
Fat: 44 g
Carbohydrates: 3 g
Fiber: 0 g
Net Carbs: 3 g

Ingredients:

2 cups heavy cream

1 vanilla bean, split and scraped (or 1 teaspoon vanilla extract)

5 large egg yolks

1/2 cup erythritol (granular), plus extra for the topping

Boiling water (for the water bath)

1. **Preheat Oven and Prepare Ramekins:**
   - Preheat the oven to 325°F (163°C).
   - Place four ramekins in a large baking dish.

2. **Infuse the Cream:** In a medium saucepan, combine the heavy cream and the scraped vanilla bean (pod and seeds). Slowly bring to a simmer over medium heat, then remove from heat and let stand for 15 minutes to infuse the vanilla flavor. If using vanilla extract, add it after removing the cream from the heat.

3. **Mix Egg Yolks and Sweetener:** In a mixing bowl, whisk the egg yolks and 1/2 cup erythritol until well combined and slightly thickened.

4. **Combine Cream and Yolk Mixture:** Slowly add the warm cream to the egg yolk mixture, stirring constantly to avoid cooking the eggs.

5. **Bake in Water Bath:**
   - Strain the mixture through a fine sieve into a pouring jug to remove the vanilla pod and any cooked egg bits.
   - Pour the strained mixture into the ramekins, dividing evenly.
   - Pour boiling water into the baking dish until it reaches halfway up the sides of the ramekins.
   - Bake for about 30-35 minutes, or until the centers are just set but still slightly wobbly.

6. **Chill:** Remove the ramekins from the water bath and let them cool to room temperature. Chill in the refrigerator for at least 2 hours, up to overnight.

7. **Caramelize the Top:**
   - Sprinkle a thin layer of erythritol over each chilled crème brûlée.
   - Use a kitchen torch to caramelize the sugar. Hold the torch about 6 inches away from the surface, moving it around until the sugar melts and forms a crispy top.

8. **Serve:** Allow the crème brûlée to sit for a few minutes before serving to let the sugar harden.

Snickerdoodles

Yield:
18 cookies

Prep Time:
15 minutes

Cook Time:
12 minutes

Total Time:
27 minutes

Nutritional Information
(per cookie):

🔥 **Calories: 110**

Protein: 3 g
Fat: 9 g
Carbohydrates: 4 g
Fiber: 2 g
Net Carbs: 2 g

Ingredients:

For the cookies:
2 cups almond flour
1/2 cup coconut flour
1/2 cup erythritol (granular)
1/4 cup butter, softened
1 large egg
1 teaspoon cream of tartar

1/2 teaspoon baking soda
1/4 teaspoon salt
2 teaspoons vanilla extract
For the cinnamon-sugar topping:
2 tablespoons erythritol (granular)
1 tablespoon ground cinnamon

1. **Preheat Oven and Prepare Baking Sheet:**
   - Preheat your oven to 350°F (175°C). Line a baking sheet with parchment paper or a silicone baking mat.

2. **Mix Cookie Dough:**
   - In a large mixing bowl, cream together the butter and 1/2 cup erythritol until light and fluffy.
   - Beat in the egg and vanilla extract.
   - In a separate bowl, whisk together the almond flour, coconut flour, cream of tartar, baking soda, and salt.
   - Gradually mix the dry ingredients into the wet ingredients until well combined. The dough should be thick and pliable.

3. **Prepare Cinnamon-Sugar Topping:**
   - In a small bowl, mix together the 2 tablespoons of erythritol and the ground cinnamon.

4. **Shape and Coat Cookies:**
   - Scoop out about 1 tablespoon of dough and roll it into a ball.
   - Roll each dough ball in the cinnamon-sugar mixture until well coated.
   - Place the coated balls on the prepared baking sheet, spacing them about 2 inches apart.

5. **Bake:**
   - Bake in the preheated oven for 10-12 minutes, or until the edges are just beginning to brown but the centers are still soft.
   - Remove from the oven and let them cool on the baking sheet for 5 minutes before transferring to a wire rack to cool completely.

Chocolate Chip Cookies

Yield:
24 cookies

Prep Time:
10 minutes

Cook Time:
12 minutes

Total Time:
22 minutes

Nutritional Information
(per cookie):

🔥 **Calories: 130**

Protein: 3 g
Fat: 11 g
Carbohydrates: 4 g
Fiber: 2 g
Net Carbs: 2 g

Ingredients:

For the cookies:

2 cups almond flour

1/4 cup coconut flour

1/2 cup erythritol (granular)

1/2 cup butter, softened

1 large egg

1 teaspoon vanilla extract

1/2 teaspoon baking soda

1/4 teaspoon salt

1/2 cup sugar-free chocolate chips

1. **Preheat Oven and Prepare Baking Sheet:**
   - Preheat your oven to 350°F (175°C). Line a baking sheet with parchment paper.

2. **Mix Cookie Dough:**
   - In a large mixing bowl, cream together the butter and erythritol until light and fluffy.
   - Beat in the egg and vanilla extract.
   - In a separate bowl, combine the almond flour, coconut flour, baking soda, and salt.
   - Gradually add the dry ingredients to the wet ingredients, mixing until well combined.
   - Fold in the sugar-free chocolate chips.

3. **Shape Cookies:**
   - Scoop out about 1 tablespoon of dough and roll it into a ball. Place the balls on the prepared baking sheet, spacing them about 2 inches apart.
   - Gently flatten each ball slightly with your fingers.

4. **Bake:**
   - Bake in the preheated oven for 10-12 minutes or until the edges are golden brown but the centers are still soft.
   - Remove from the oven and let them cool on the baking sheet for 5 minutes before transferring to a wire rack to cool completely.

Macadamia Nut Blondies

Yield:
12 servings

Prep Time:
10 minutes

Cook Time:
25 minutes

Total Time:
35 minutes

Nutritional Information
(per serving):

🔥 **Calories: 200**

Protein: 4 g
Fat: 18 g
Carbohydrates: 6 g
Fiber: 3 g
Net Carbs: 3 g

Ingredients:
For the blondies:
1 cup almond flour
1/2 cup coconut flour
1/3 cup erythritol (granular)
1/2 teaspoon baking powder
1/4 teaspoon salt

1/2 cup butter, melted
2 large eggs
1 teaspoon vanilla extract
1/2 cup macadamia nuts, roughly chopped
Optional: 1/4 cup sugar-free chocolate chips

1. **Preheat Oven and Prepare Pan:**
   - Preheat your oven to 350°F (175°C). Line an 8-inch square baking pan with parchment paper, allowing excess to hang over the sides for easy removal.

2. **Mix Dry Ingredients:**
   - In a large bowl, whisk together almond flour, coconut flour, erythritol, baking powder, and salt.

3. **Combine Wet Ingredients:**
   - In another bowl, mix together the melted butter, eggs, and vanilla extract until well combined.

4. **Combine Wet and Dry Ingredients:**
   - Add the wet ingredients to the dry ingredients and stir until just combined. Fold in the chopped macadamia nuts and, if using, the sugar-free chocolate chips.

5. **Bake:**
   - Spread the batter evenly into the prepared pan.
   - Bake for 25 minutes, or until the top is golden and a toothpick inserted into the center comes out clean or with just a few crumbs.

6. **Cool and Serve:**
   - Let the blondies cool in the pan on a wire rack before lifting out using the parchment paper. Cut into 12 squares.

Lemon Pound Cake

Yield:
12 servings

Prep Time:
15 minutes

Cook Time:
45 minutes

Total Time:
1 hour

Nutritional Information
(per serving,
without glaze):

🔥 **Calories: 280**

Protein: 8 g
Fat: 24 g
Carbohydrates: 8 g
Fiber: 3 g
Net Carbs: 5 g

Ingredients:

For the cake:
2 1/2 cups almond flour
1/2 cup coconut flour
1 cup erythritol (granular)
2 teaspoons baking powder
1/4 teaspoon salt
1/2 cup unsalted butter, softened

4 large eggs
1/2 cup sour cream
1/4 cup fresh lemon juice
Zest of 2 lemons
For the glaze (optional):
1/4 cup powdered erythritol
1-2 tablespoons lemon juice

1. **Preheat Oven and Prepare Pan:**
   - Preheat your oven to 350°F (175°C). Grease and flour a loaf pan with a bit of coconut flour or line it with parchment paper.

2. **Mix Dry Ingredients:**
   - In a large bowl, whisk together almond flour, coconut flour, erythritol, baking powder, and salt.

3. **Cream Butter and Eggs:**
   - In another large bowl, beat the butter until creamy. Add eggs one at a time, fully incorporating each before adding the next.

4. **Combine Wet and Dry Ingredients:**
   - Mix in the sour cream, lemon juice, and lemon zest into the butter mixture.
   - Gradually add the dry ingredients to the wet ingredients, mixing until just combined to avoid over-mixing.

5. **Bake:**
   - Pour the batter into the prepared loaf pan and smooth the top.
   - Bake for 45 minutes, or until a toothpick inserted into the center comes out clean.
   - Prepare Glaze (if using):
   - While the cake cools, whisk together powdered erythritol and lemon juice to create a thick but pourable glaze.

6. **Cool and Glaze:**
   - Let the cake cool in the pan for about 10 minutes before removing to a wire rack to cool completely.
   - Drizzle the glaze over the cooled cake.

Key Lime Pie

Yield:
8 servings

Prep Time:
20 minutes

Cook Time:
10 minutes
(plus chilling time)

Total Time:
30 minutes

Nutritional Information
(per serving):

🔥 **Calories: 390**

Protein: 7 g
Fat: 36 g
Carbohydrates: 8 g
Fiber: 3 g
Net Carbs: 5 g

Ingredients:

For the crust:

1 1/2 cups almond flour

1/4 cup coconut flour

1/3 cup melted butter

1 tablespoon erythritol (granular)

For the filling:

1 cup heavy cream

8 ounces cream cheese, softened

1/2 cup key lime juice (or regular lime juice if key limes are unavailable)

Zest of 2 key limes (or regular limes)

1/2 cup erythritol (powdered)

1 teaspoon vanilla extract

1. **Prepare the crust:**
   - Preheat oven to 350°F (175°C).
   - In a mixing bowl, combine almond flour, coconut flour, melted butter, and granular erythritol until the mixture resembles coarse crumbs.
   - Press the mixture into the bottom and up the sides of a 9-inch pie plate.
   - Bake for 10 minutes or until the edges are lightly golden. Remove from oven and let cool completely.

2. **Make the filling:**
   - In a large mixing bowl, beat the heavy cream until stiff peaks form.
   - In another bowl, mix the softened cream cheese with powdered erythritol until smooth.
   - Add key lime juice, lime zest, and vanilla extract to the cream cheese mixture and mix until well combined.
   - Gently fold the whipped cream into the cream cheese mixture until fully incorporated.

3. **Assemble the pie:**
   - Pour the filling into the cooled crust and smooth the top with a spatula.
   - Chill in the refrigerator for at least 4 hours, or until set.

4. **Serve:**
   - Garnish with additional lime zest or lime slices before serving, if desired.

Almond Joy Bars

Yield:
16 bars

Prep Time:
20 minutes

Cook Time:
5 minutes
(plus chilling time)

Total Time:
25 minutes

Nutritional Information
(per bar):

🔥 **Calories: 180**

Protein: 2 g
Fat: 16 g
Carbohydrates: 5 g
Fiber: 3 g
Net Carbs: 2 g

Ingredients:

For the coconut layer:

2 cups unsweetened shredded coconut

1/2 cup coconut cream

1/4 cup erythritol (powdered)

1 teaspoon vanilla extract

For the almond layer:

16 whole almonds

For the chocolate layer:

1/2 cup sugar-free dark chocolate chips

1 tablespoon coconut oil

1. **Prepare the coconut layer:**
   - In a medium bowl, combine the shredded coconut, coconut cream, powdered erythritol, and vanilla extract. Mix until all the coconut is moistened and the mixture holds together when squeezed.
   - Press the coconut mixture into the bottom of a lined 8x8-inch baking dish, creating an even layer.

2. **Add the almonds:**
   - Place one whole almond in a regular pattern on top of the pressed coconut layer, embedding each slightly into the coconut.

3. **Prepare the chocolate layer:**
   - In a small saucepan over low heat, melt the chocolate chips and coconut oil together, stirring until smooth.
   - Pour the melted chocolate over the coconut and almond layers, spreading it out to cover the surface evenly.

4. **Chill the bars:**
   - Refrigerate the tray for at least 2 hours or until the chocolate is firm and the coconut layer is set.

5. **Serve:**
   - Once chilled, lift the bars out of the tray using the edges of the lining. Cut into 16 squares.

Biscotti

Yield:
24 biscotti

Prep Time:
15 minutes

Cook Time:
45 minutes

Total Time:
1 hour

Nutritional Information
(per biscotti):

🔥 **Calories: 90**

Protein: 3 g
Fat: 7 g
Carbohydrates: 3 g
Fiber: 1 g
Net Carbs: 2 g

Ingredients:

For the biscotti:

2 1/2 cups almond flour

1/2 cup erythritol (granular)

1 teaspoon baking powder

1/2 teaspoon xanthan gum (optional, for texture)

1/4 teaspoon salt

3 large eggs

1 teaspoon vanilla extract

1/2 cup sliced almonds

Optional: Zest of 1 orange or lemon for added flavor

1. **Preheat Oven and Prepare Baking Sheet:**
   - Preheat your oven to 325°F (163°C). Line a baking sheet with parchment paper.

2. **Mix Dry Ingredients:**
   - In a large bowl, combine almond flour, erythritol, baking powder, xanthan gum (if using), and salt. Mix well to distribute all the ingredients evenly.

3. **Add Wet Ingredients:**
   - In a separate bowl, whisk the eggs and vanilla extract. Add the egg mixture to the dry ingredients, mixing until a dough forms. Stir in the sliced almonds and citrus zest (if using).

4. **Shape and Bake the Dough:**
   - Divide the dough into two equal parts. Shape each part into a log approximately 12 inches long and 2 inches wide. Place the logs on the prepared baking sheet.
   - Bake for 25 minutes, or until the logs are lightly golden and firm to the touch.

5. **Slice and Second Bake:**
   - Remove from the oven and let cool for 10 minutes. Using a sharp knife, cut the logs diagonally into 1/2-inch thick slices.
   - Arrange the slices back on the baking sheet, cut side down.
   - Return to the oven and bake for an additional 10-15 minutes per side, or until the biscotti are crisp and golden.

6. **Cool and Serve:**
   - Let the biscotti cool completely on a wire rack. They will continue to crisp as they cool.

CHAPTER 9

Bulletproof beverages

Bulletproof Coffee

Yield:
1 serving

Prep time:
5 minutes

Cook time:
0 minutes

Total Time:
5 minutes

Nutritional Information
(per serving):

🔥 **Calories: 220**

Protein: 0 g | Fat: 24 g | Carbohydrates: 0 g | Fiber: 0 g | Net Carbs: 0 g

Ingredients:

1 cup (240 ml) hot brewed coffee (preferably from quality, low-toxin coffee beans)

1 tablespoon (15 ml) MCT oil or coconut oil

1 tablespoon (15 g) unsalted butter or ghee (grass-fed preferred)

Optional: sweetener such as stevia or erythritol, to taste

Optional: a pinch of cinnamon or vanilla extract for flavor

1. **Brew Coffee:** Brew one cup of coffee using your preferred method. Freshly brewed coffee is best for flavor and warmth.

2. **Combine Ingredients:** Pour the hot coffee into a blender. Add the MCT oil or coconut oil and the butter or ghee.

3. **Blend:** Blend on high speed for 20 to 30 seconds until the mixture is smooth and creamy, with a frothy top.

4. **Serve:** Pour the coffee into a mug. If desired, add a sweetener like stevia or erythritol and a pinch of cinnamon or vanilla extract for enhanced flavor.

Iced Matcha Latte

Yield:
1 serving

Prep time:
5 minutes

Cook time:
0 minutes

Total Time:
5 minutes

Nutritional Information
(per serving):

🔥 **Calories: 70**
(without MCT oil)

Protein: 1 g | Fat: 4 g (9 g with MCT oil) | Carbohydrates: 1 g | Fiber: 0 g | Net Carbs: 1 g

Ingredients:

1 teaspoon matcha green tea powder

1/4 cup hot water (not boiling)

3/4 cup unsweetened almond milk

1 tablespoon MCT oil or coconut oil (optional for added fat)

Sweetener to taste (e.g., erythritol, stevia)

Ice cubes

1. **Dissolve Matcha:** Sift the matcha powder into a small bowl to remove any lumps. Add the hot water and whisk vigorously until the matcha is fully dissolved and there is a light froth on top.

2. **Mix with Almond Milk:** In a shaker or blender, combine the dissolved matcha with the almond milk, MCT oil (if using), and your choice of sweetener.

3. **Add Ice and Serve:** Fill a glass with ice cubes. Pour the matcha mixture over the ice. Stir well to ensure everything is combined.

4. **Garnish and Enjoy:** Optionally, you can sprinkle a little matcha powder on top for garnish. Serve immediately for the best flavor.

Chocolate Avocado Smoothie

 Yield:
1 serving

 Prep time:
5 minutes

 Cook time:
0 minutes

 Total Time:
5 minutes

Nutritional Information
(per serving):

🔥 **Calories: 345**

Protein: 4 g | Fat: 29 g |
Carbohydrates: 18 g | Fiber:
9 g | Net Carbs: 9 g

Ingredients:

1 medium avocado, peeled and pitted

2 tablespoons unsweetened cocoa powder

1 cup unsweetened almond milk

1 tablespoon MCT oil or coconut oil

1/2 teaspoon vanilla extract

Sweetener to taste (e.g., stevia, erythritol)

Ice cubes (optional, for a thicker smoothie)

1. **Combine Ingredients:** In a blender, combine the avocado, cocoa powder, almond milk, MCT oil, vanilla extract, and your choice of sweetener.

2. **Blend:** Add a few ice cubes if you prefer a thicker, colder smoothie. Blend on high until smooth and creamy.

3. **Adjust and Serve:**

   - Taste the smoothie and adjust the sweetness if necessary. If the smoothie is too thick, you can thin it by adding a little more almond milk.

   - Pour the smoothie into a glass and serve immediately.

Turmeric Tea (Golden Milk)

 Yield:
2 servings

 Prep time:
5 minutes

 Cook time:
10 minutes

 Total Time:
15 minutes

Nutritional Information
(per serving):

🔥 **Calories: 240**

Protein: 2 g | Fat: 24 g |
Carbohydrates: 3 g | Fiber:
1 g | Net Carbs: 2 g

Ingredients:

2 cups coconut milk (full-fat for creaminess)

1 teaspoon turmeric powder

1/2 teaspoon cinnamon powder

1/4 teaspoon ginger powder

A pinch of black pepper (to enhance turmeric absorption)

Sweetener to taste (e.g., erythritol or stevia)

1 tablespoon coconut oil or MCT oil (optional, for added fat)

1. **Heat Ingredients:** In a small saucepan, combine the coconut milk, turmeric powder, cinnamon, ginger, and black pepper. Heat over medium heat until the mixture is hot but not boiling, stirring occasionally to ensure the spices are well mixed.

2. **Add Fats and Sweetener:** Reduce the heat to low and stir in the coconut oil or MCT oil if using. Add sweetener to taste, adjusting based on your preference for sweetness.

3. **Simmer:** Allow the mixture to simmer gently for about 10 minutes. This will help the flavors to meld and intensify.

4. **Serve:** Strain the mixture through a fine mesh sieve into two cups to remove any large spice particles. Serve warm.

Strawberry Coconut Milkshake

Yield:
2 servings

Prep Time:
5 minutes

Cook Time:
0 minutes

Total Time:
5 minutes

Nutritional Information
(per serving):

🔥 Calories: 230

Protein: 2 g
Fat: 22 g
Carbohydrates: 7 g
Fiber: 2 g
Net Carbs: 5 g

Ingredients:

1 cup strawberries (fresh or frozen)

1 cup coconut milk (full-fat for creaminess)

1/2 cup ice cubes

Sweetener to taste (e.g., erythritol or stevia)

1 teaspoon vanilla extract

Optional: 1 tablespoon MCT oil for added ketones and energy

1. **Prepare Ingredients:**
   - If using fresh strawberries, wash and hull them. If using frozen, ensure they are slightly thawed for easier blending.

2. **Blend Ingredients:**
   - In a blender, combine the strawberries, coconut milk, ice cubes, sweetener, vanilla extract, and MCT oil if using. Blend on high until smooth and creamy.

3. **Adjust Consistency and Taste:**
   - If the milkshake is too thick, you can add a bit more coconut milk to adjust the consistency. Taste and add more sweetener if needed.

4. **Serve:**
   - Pour the milkshake into glasses and serve immediately. You can garnish with a few slices of strawberry or a sprinkle of shredded coconut for a decorative touch.

CHAPTER 10

Sauces

Mayonnaise

Yield:
About 1 cup

Prep Time:
10 minutes

Cook Time:
0 minutes

Total Time:
10 minutes

Nutritional Information
(per tablespoon approximately):

🔥 **Calories: 100**

Total Fat: 11g
Saturated Fat: 1.5g
Trans Fat: 0g
Cholesterol: 10mg
Sodium: 50mg
Total Carbohydrates: 0.1g
Dietary Fiber: 0g
Sugars: 0g
Protein: 0.2g

Ingredients:

1 large egg, at room temperature

1 tablespoon Dijon mustard

1 tablespoon apple cider vinegar

1 cup light olive oil or avocado oil

Salt to taste

Optional: A pinch of ground black pepper or a few drops of stevia for sweetness

1. **Combine Egg and Condiments:**
   - In a blender or food processor, combine the egg, Dijon mustard, and apple cider vinegar. Blend them together until the mixture is smooth.

2. **Emulsify with Oil:**
   - With the blender on a low setting, slowly drizzle in the oil. This process should be gradual to ensure that the oil fully integrates with the egg mixture, creating a thick and creamy emulsion.

3. **Season:**
   - Once all the oil has been added and the mixture has thickened, add salt to taste. If using, add pepper or stevia and blend briefly to incorporate.

4. **Taste and Adjust:**
   - Taste the mayonnaise and adjust the seasoning if needed. If the mayonnaise is too thick, you can thin it by whisking in a teaspoon of water.

5. **Store:**
   - Transfer the mayonnaise to a jar with a lid and refrigerate. It should keep well for about a week.

This simple recipe for homemade keto mayonnaise, which is great for those following a low-carb diet. This recipe will provide a rich, creamy mayo that's perfect for salads, sandwiches, and various keto dishes.

Pesto

Yield:
About 1 cup

Prep Time:
10 minutes

Cook Time:
0 minutes

Total Time:
10 minutes

Nutritional Information
(per tablespoon approximately):

🔥 **Calories: 100**

Total Fat: 10g
Saturated Fat: 2g
Cholesterol: 4mg
Sodium: 75mg
Total Carbohydrates: 1g
Dietary Fiber: 0.5g
Sugars: 0.2g
Protein: 2g

Ingredients:

2 cups fresh basil leaves, packed

1/3 cup pine nuts (or substitute with walnuts for a different flavor)

3 cloves garlic, peeled

1/2 cup grated Parmesan cheese

1/2 cup extra-virgin olive oil

Salt and pepper, to taste

Optional: 1 tablespoon lemon juice for added zest

1. **Prepare Ingredients:**
   - Wash the basil leaves and pat dry. Lightly toast the pine nuts in a skillet over medium heat until they are golden and fragrant, being careful not to burn them.

2. **Blend Base Ingredients:**
   - In a food processor, combine the basil leaves, toasted pine nuts, and garlic cloves. Pulse until coarsely chopped.

3. **Add Cheese and Oil:**
   - Add the grated Parmesan cheese to the food processor. With the processor running, slowly drizzle in the olive oil until the mixture is well combined and reaches your desired consistency.

4. **Season:**
   - Season with salt and pepper to taste. If using, add the lemon juice and blend briefly to incorporate.

5. **Storage:**
   - Transfer the pesto into a jar or an airtight container. If not using immediately, pour a thin layer of olive oil over the top to help pre-serve the green color. Refrigerate and use within a week, or freeze for up to 3 months.

This pesto is rich in healthy fats and full of flavor, making it a perfect addition to your low-carb meals. Enjoy it with zucchini noodles, as a flavorful topping for grilled meats, or simply as a dip!

Alfredo Sauce

Yield:
About 2 cups

Prep Time:
5 minutes

Cook Time:
10 minutes

Total Time:
15 minutes

Nutritional Information
(per 1/4 cup serving
approximately):

🔥 Calories: 260

Total Fat: 25g
Saturated Fat: 16g
Cholesterol: 85mg
Sodium: 320mg
Total Carbohydrates: 2g
Dietary Fiber: 0g
Sugars: 1g
Protein: 7g

Ingredients:

1 cup heavy cream

1/2 cup unsalted butter

1 clove garlic, minced

1 1/2 cups grated Parmesan cheese

1/4 teaspoon ground black pepper

Salt to taste

Optional: Nutmeg for seasoning

1. **Melt Butter:**
   - In a medium saucepan, melt the butter over medium heat. Add the minced garlic and sauté for about 1 minute until fragrant, but not browned.

2. **Add Cream:**
   - Pour in the heavy cream and bring the mixture to a simmer, stirring frequently.

3. **Incorporate Cheese:**
   - Lower the heat and gradually add the grated Parmesan cheese to the cream mixture. Stir continuously until the cheese is fully melted and the sauce is smooth and creamy.

4. **Season:**
   - Season with ground black pepper and a pinch of salt. If using, add a small pinch of nutmeg for extra flavor. Adjust the seasoning as needed.

5. **Serve or Store:**
   - Use the Alfredo sauce immediately over your favorite keto-friendly dishes, or let it cool and store in an airtight container in the refrigerator for up to one week. Reheat gently while stirring to maintain the creamy texture.

This sauce is low in carbs, making it perfect for those on a ketogenic diet. It pairs beautifully with zucchini noodles, grilled chicken, or as a decadent sauce for vegetables.

Guacamole

Yield:
About 2 cups

Prep Time:
10 minutes

Cook Time:
0 minutes

Total Time:
10 minutes

Nutritional Information
(per 1/4 cup serving
approximately):

🔥 **Calories: 120**

Total Fat: 10g
Saturated Fat: 1.5g
Cholesterol: 0mg
Sodium: 5mg
Total Carbohydrates: 8g
Dietary Fiber: 5g
Sugars: 1g
Protein: 2g

Ingredients:

3 medium ripe avocados, peeled and pitted

1 small red onion, finely chopped

2 Roma tomatoes, seeded and diced

1 jalapeño pepper, seeded and finely chopped (optional)

1/4 cup fresh cilantro, chopped

Juice of 1 lime

Salt and pepper to taste

Optional: 1 clove garlic, minced

1. **Mash Avocados:**
   - In a medium bowl, use a fork or potato masher to mash the avocados to your desired consistency—smooth or chunky.

2. **Add Fresh Ingredients:**
   - Stir in the chopped red onion, diced tomatoes, jalapeño (if using) and cilantro. Mix well to combine all the ingredients.

3. **Flavor with Lime and Seasonings:**
   - Squeeze in the lime juice, and add the minced garlic if using. Season with salt and pepper to taste. Mix everything together until well combined.

4. **Taste and Adjust:**
   - Taste your guacamole and adjust the seasoning if necessary. If you like it a bit more acidic, you can add more lime juice.

5. **Serve or Store:**
   - Serve immediately with keto-friendly chips or cut vegetables. If storing, place plastic wrap directly on the surface of the guacamole to prevent oxidation and refrigerate. Use within 24 hours for best quality.

This keto guacamole is not only flavorful but also beneficial for a ketogenic diet, focusing on high healthy fats and low net carbs. Enjoy this guacamole as a dip, spread, or salad topping to enhance your meals with a fresh, zesty touch!

Chimichurri

Yield:
About 1 cup

Prep Time:
10 minutes

Cook Time:
0 minutes

Total Time:
10 minutes

Nutritional Information
(per tablespoon approximately):

🔥 Calories: 80

Total Fat: 8g
Saturated Fat: 1g
Cholesterol: 0mg
Sodium: 75mg
Total Carbohydrates: 1g
Dietary Fiber: 0.3g
Sugars: 0.2g
Protein: 0.2g

Ingredients:

1 cup fresh flat-leaf parsley, tightly packed and finely chopped

4 cloves garlic, minced

1/4 cup fresh oregano leaves, finely chopped

1/2 cup extra virgin olive oil

2 tablespoons red wine vinegar

1 teaspoon red pepper flakes (adjust to taste)

1/2 teaspoon salt

1/4 teaspoon freshly ground black pepper

1. **Prepare the Herbs:**
   - Wash and dry the parsley and oregano leaves thoroughly. Finely chop the herbs and place them in a medium bowl.

2. **Add Garlic and Seasonings:**
   - Add the minced garlic, red pepper flakes, salt, and black pepper to the herbs.

3. **Mix with Liquids:**
   - Pour in the olive oil and red wine vinegar. Stir all the ingredients together until well combined.

4. **Let It Marinate:**
   - Allow the chimichurri to sit for at least 10 minutes before serving to let the flavors meld together. For best results, let it sit for a few hours or overnight in the refrigerator.

5. **Serve or Store:**
   - Serve immediately or store in an airtight container in the refrigerator for up to a week. The flavors will continue to develop and improve over time.

This vibrant and flavorful recipe for homemade Keto Chimichurri, an Argentinean sauce that pairs exceptionally well with grilled meats and vegetables. This sauce is naturally low in carbohydrates and high in healthy fats, making it perfect for a ketogenic diet.

Caesar Dressing

Yield:
About 1 cup

Prep Time:
10 minutes

Cook Time:
0 minutes

Total Time:
10 minutes

Nutritional Information
(per tablespoon approximately):

🔥 **Calories: 100**

Total Fat: 10g
Saturated Fat: 2g
Cholesterol: 10mg
Sodium: 180mg
Total Carbohydrates: 0.5g
Dietary Fiber: 0g
Sugars: 0g
Protein: 1g

Ingredients:

3/4 cup mayonnaise (preferably made with avocado oil)

1/4 cup grated Parmesan cheese

1 tablespoon lemon juice

1 teaspoon Dijon mustard

1 teaspoon Worcestershire sauce (ensure it's sugar-free for keto)

2 cloves garlic, minced

2 anchovy fillets, minced (or use 1 teaspoon anchovy paste)

Salt and pepper to taste

1. **Combine Ingredients:**
   - In a blender or food processor, combine the mayonnaise, grated Parmesan cheese, lemon juice, Dijon mustard, Worcestershire sauce, minced garlic, and anchovy fillets.

2. **Blend:**
   - Blend all the ingredients until smooth and creamy. If the dressing is too thick, you can thin it by adding a few teaspoons of water until you reach the desired consistency.

3. **Season:**
   - Taste the dressing and season with salt and pepper as needed. Remember that anchovies and Parmesan are salty, so add salt cautiously.

4. **Chill:**
   - Transfer the dressing to an airtight container and refrigerate for at least an hour before serving. This allows the flavors to meld together beautifully.

5. **Serve:**
   - Use this dressing on your favorite keto salads, as a dip for vegetables, or as a sauce for grilled meats.

This recipe for a creamy and delicious Keto Caesar Dressing that's perfect for dressing up salads while keeping it low carb. This dressing offers the classic Caesar taste without any added sugars, making it ideal for a ketogenic lifestyle.

Worcestershire Sauce

Yield:
About 1 cup

Prep Time:
5 minutes

Cook Time:
20 minutes

Total Time:
25 minutes

Nutritional Information
(per tablespoon
approximately):

🔥 **Calories: 5**

Total Fat: 0g
Saturated Fat: 0g
Cholesterol: 0mg
Sodium: 150mg
Total Carbohydrates: 1g
Dietary Fiber: 0g
Sugars: 0g
Protein: 0g

Ingredients:

1/2 cup apple cider vinegar

2 tablespoons water

2 tablespoons soy sauce or tamari (ensure gluten-free if necessary)

1 tablespoon lemon juice

1 tablespoon fish sauce

2 teaspoons mustard powder

1 teaspoon onion powder

1 teaspoon garlic powder

1/2 teaspoon ground ginger

1/2 teaspoon ground cinnamon

1/4 teaspoon black pepper

2 cloves, ground

Optional: 1/4 teaspoon liquid smoke for added depth

1. **Combine Ingredients:**
   - In a small saucepan, combine all the ingredients listed. Stir well to ensure that all the spices are fully dissolved and mixed.

2. **Simmer:**
   - Place the saucepan over medium heat and bring the mixture to a simmer. Reduce the heat to low and let it simmer gently for about 20 minutes. Stir occasionally to prevent sticking and to ensure that the flavors meld together.

3. **Cool and Strain:**
   - After simmering, remove the saucepan from the heat and allow the sauce to cool slightly. Strain the mixture through a fine mesh sieve to remove any solids and achieve a smooth texture.

4. **Bottle and Store:**
   - Transfer the strained sauce into a clean bottle or jar. Seal and store in the refrigerator. The sauce will keep for up to a month.

This homemade Keto Worcestershire Sauce adds a aroma of soups, stews, and sauces, enhancing your dishes without adding any unnecessary carbs or sugars. Enjoy this versatile condiment as part of your keto cooking repertoire!

CHAPTER 11

30-day meal plan

DAY	BREAKFAST	LUNCH	DINNER	DESSERT
1	Spinach, mushrooms, tomatoes, avocado, scrambled eggs	Crispy Salmon with Broccoli & Bell Pepper	Lamb Chops with Rosemary and Garlic	Cheesecake
2	Turkey Bacon & Spinach Crepes	Dilled Salmon in Creamy Sauce	Meatballs	Chocolate Mousse
3	Eggs with prosciutto wrapped asparagus	Baked Cod with Parmesan and Almonds	Pork Schnitzel	Brownies
4	Chocolate Keto Omelet	Pan-Seared Lemon-Garlic Salmon	Italian Stuffed Bell Peppers	Lemon Bars
5	Cheese and onion cheesecakes	Tuna Salad	Bacon-Wrapped Pork Tenderloin	Peanut Butter Cookies
6	Almond Keto Porridge	Fish Tacos	Almond and Caraway Crust Steak	Tiramisu
7	Frittata with goat cheese and mushrooms	Seafood Chowder	Almond Butter Beef Stew	Coconut Flour Pancakes
8	Avocado and egg salad	Pan-Seared Tuna Steak	Beef Burgers with Lettuce & Avocado	Ice Cream
9	Chia seed pudding	Spicy Tuna Stuffed Avocados	Garlic Pork Chops with Mint Pesto	Chocolate Cake
10	Cauliflower Hash Browns	Sushi Rolls	Ground beef stew with Majoram & Basil	Pumpkin Pie
11	Sausage and Pepper Skillet	Crab Cakes	Cider-Herb Pork Tenderloin	Vanilla Cupcakes
12	Breakfast Sandwich	Grilled Octopus with Olive Oil and Lemon	Coconut-Olive Beef with Mushrooms	Pecan Pie
13	Herbet Buttery Breakfast Steak	Parmesan Shrimp Scampi Pizza	Beef Ragout with Pepper & Greens Beans	Creme Brulee
14	Low-Carb Smoothie Bowl	Spicy Keto Fish Stew	Sausage & Zucchini Lazagna	Snickerdoodles

DAY	BREAKFAST	LUNCH	DINNER	DESSERT
15	Savory Waffles with Cheese & Tomato	Lemon Garlic Mussels	Creamy Pork Chops	Chocolate Chip Cookies
16	Baked Avocado Eggs	Chicken Parmesan	Lamb Curry	Macadamia Nut Blondies
17	Cottage Cheese Bowls	Buffalo Chicken Stuffed Peppers	Lamb Meatballs with Feta Cheese	Lemon Pound Cake
18	Bacon-Wrapped Avocado	Creamy Tuscan Garlic Chicken	Spiced Ground Lamb with Cauliflower Rice	Key Lime Pie
19	Pumpkin Spice Keto Porridge	Spinach and Feta Stuffed Chicken	Beef and Broccoli Stir-Fry	Almond Joy Bars
20	Zucchini and Herb Breakfast Muffins	Chicken Salad	Beef Stuffed Zucchini Boats	Biscotti
21	Cream Cheese Pancakes	Lemon Herb Roasted Chicken	Chicken Bacon Ranch Casserole	Cheesecake
22	Smoked Salmon and Cream Cheese Roll-Ups	Chicken Tenders	Spinach Artichoke heart chicken	Chocolate Mousse
23	Ham and Cheese Keto Breakfast Roll-Ups	Garlic Parmesan Wings	Bacon-Wrapped Chicken Livers	Brownies
24	Garlic Butter Mushrooms with Poached Eggs	Turkey Meatballs	Chicken Liver Mousse	Lemon Bars
25	Blueberry Muffins	Chicken Liver Salad	Chicken Liver and Mushroom Bake	Peanut Butter Cookies
26	Spicy Sausage and Kale Breakfast Skillet	Chicken Liver and Mushroom Bake	Turkey Pot Pie	Tiramisu
27	Peanut Butter Keto Smoothie	Turkey Chili	Turkey Heart Pâté	Coconut Flour Pancakes
28	Lemon Poppy Seed Muffins	Turkey Heart Goulash	Turkey Liver Stroganoff	Ice Cream
29	Granola Bars	Turkey Liver Stroganoff	Chicken Parmesan	Chocolate Cake
30	Breakfast Pizza	Buffalo Chicken Stuffed Peppers	Creamy Tuscan Garlic Chicken	Pumpkin Pie

Made in United States
Orlando, FL
11 July 2024

48800844R00091